How to Draw Animals

For Beginners

40 Drawings with Step-by-Step Instructions

Copyright © 2020 by Keep 'em Busy Books

ISBN: 978-1-989842-39-3

WELCOME TO
HOW TO DRAW ANIMALS
FOR BEGINNERS.

IN THIS BOOK, YOU'LL FIND
STEP-BY-STEP INSTRUCTIONS FOR
DRAWING 40 DIFFERENT ANIMALS.

YOU'LL ALSO BE ABLE TO PRACTICE
DRAWING EACH ANIMAL ON THE
PROVIDED PAGES.

EXTRA DRAWING PAGES ARE
PROVIDED AT THE BACK OF THIS BOOK.

HAPPY DRAWING!

How to Draw a Duck

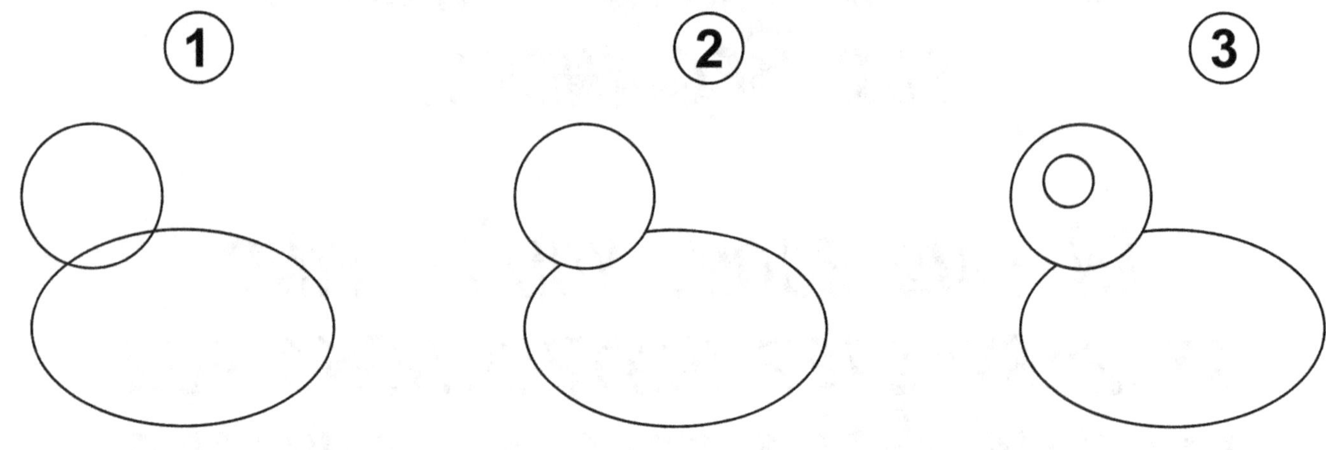

Now You Try!

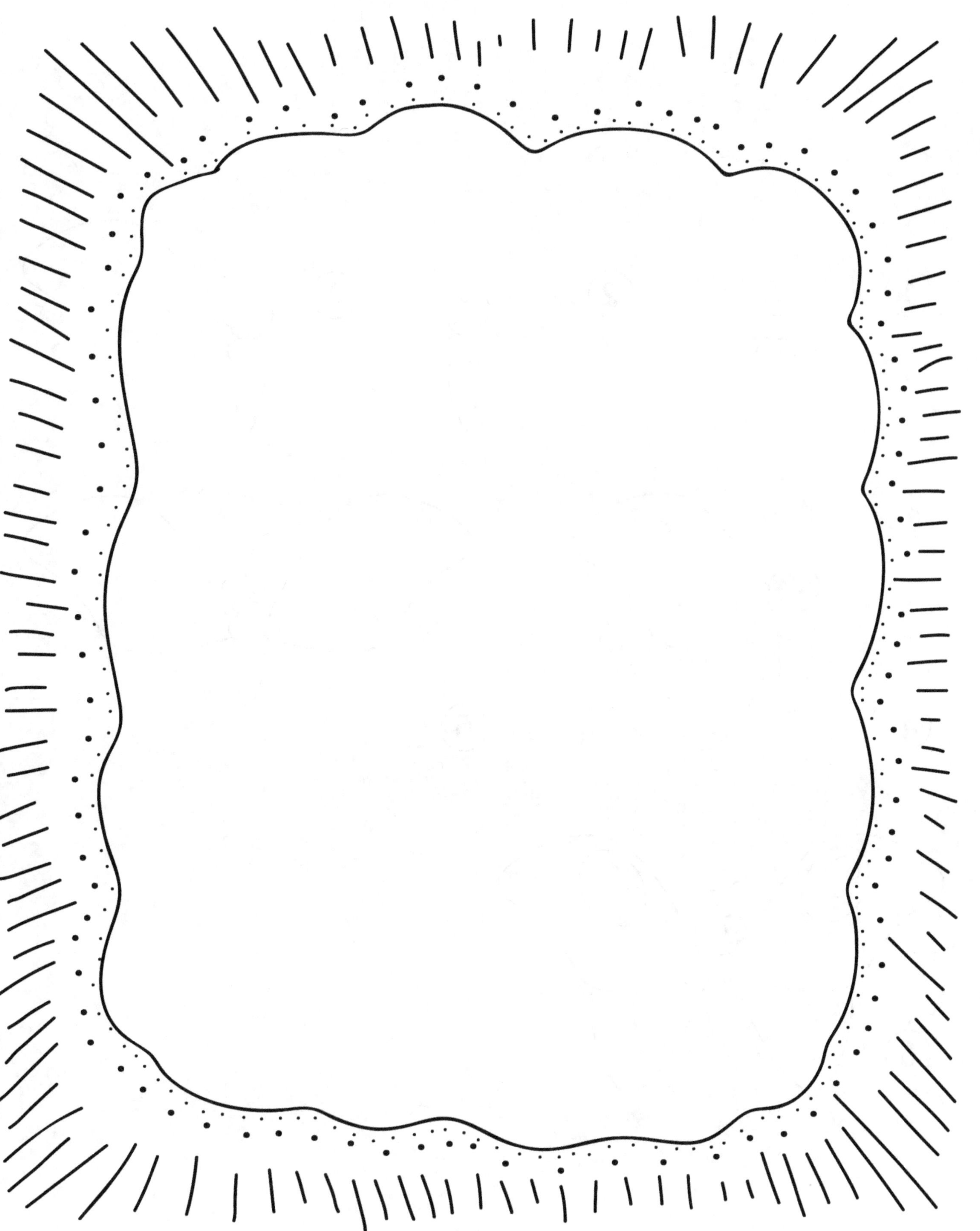

How to Draw a Butterfly

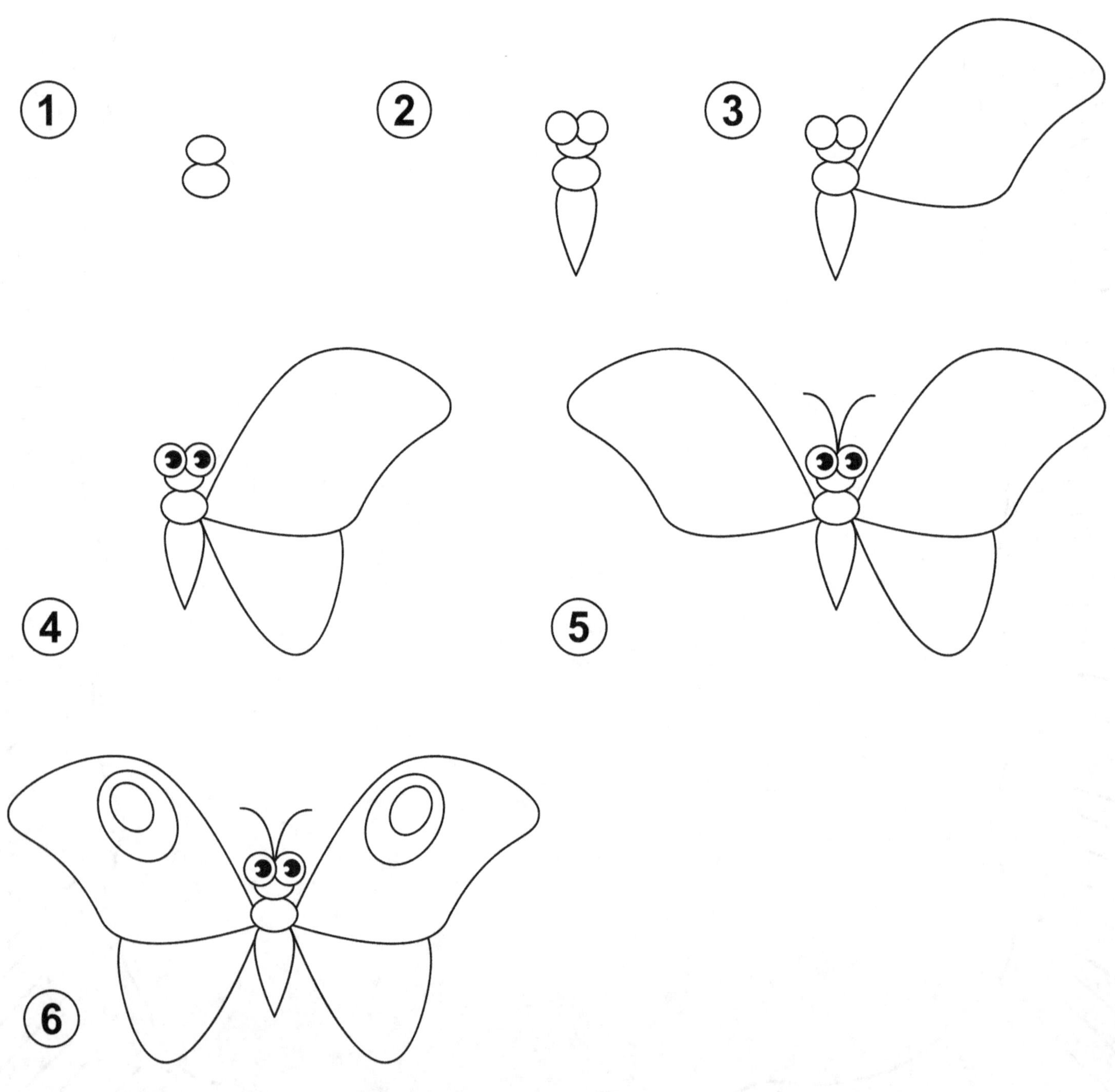

Now You Try!

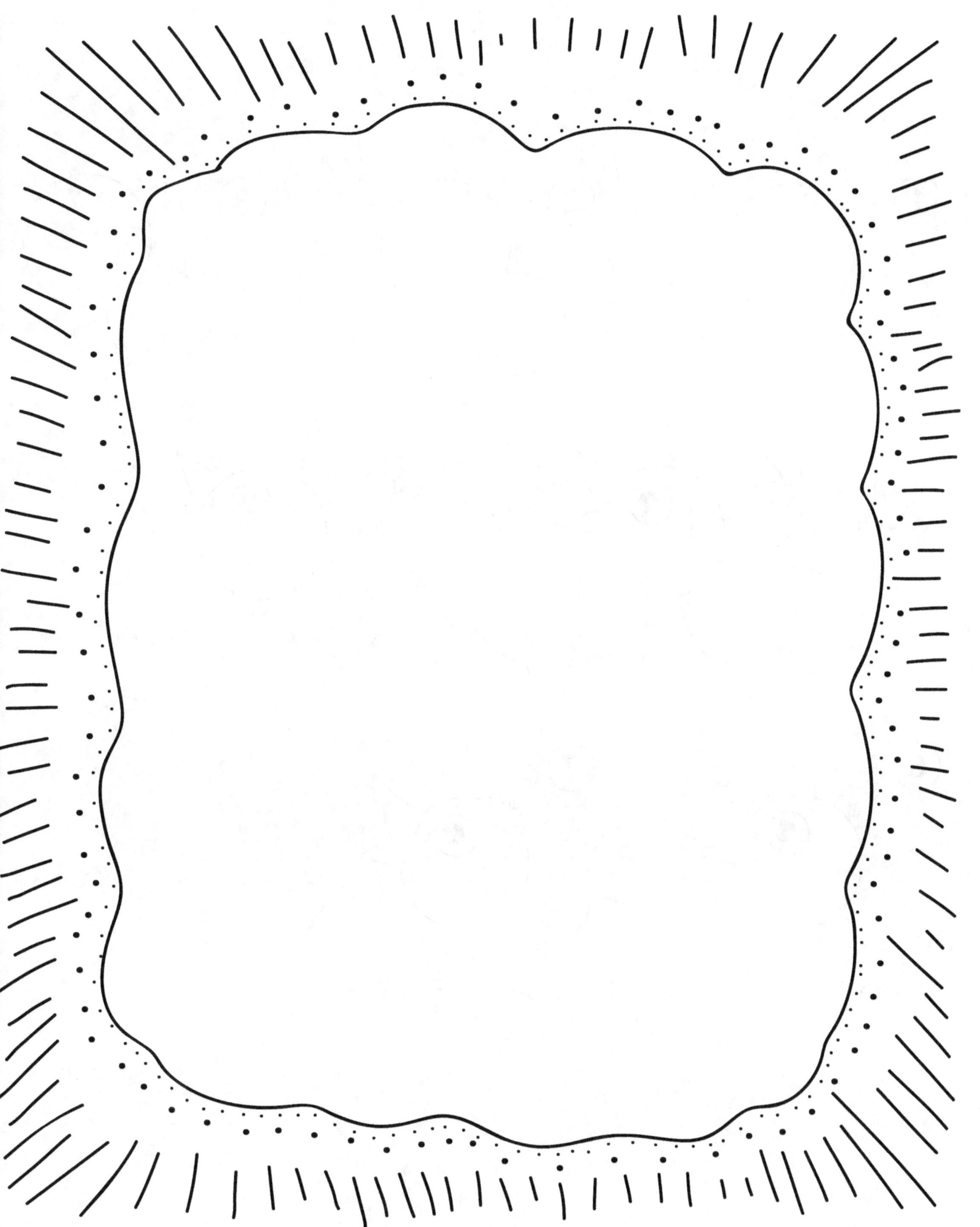

How to Draw a Bird

Now You Try!

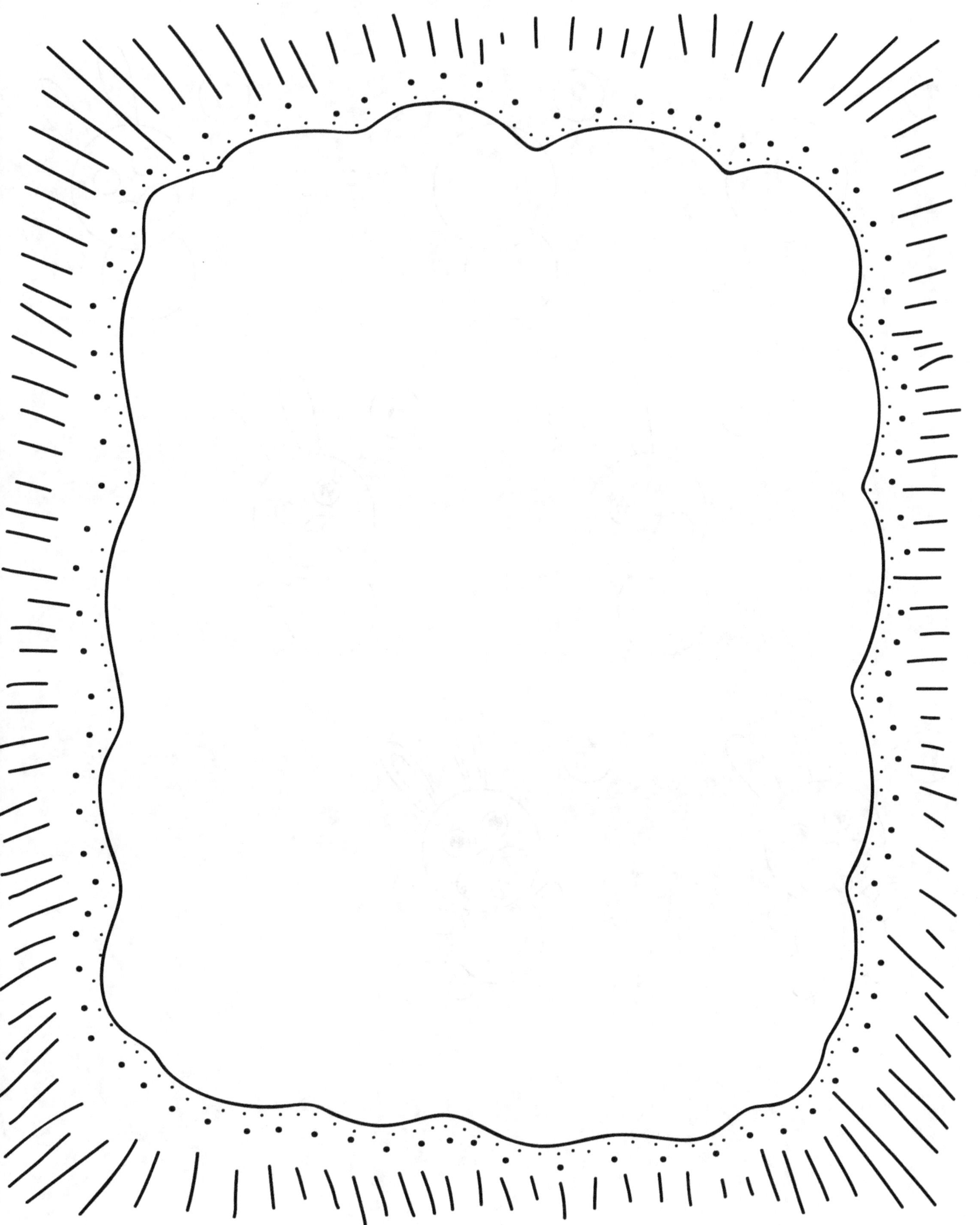

How to Draw a Rabbit

Now You Try!

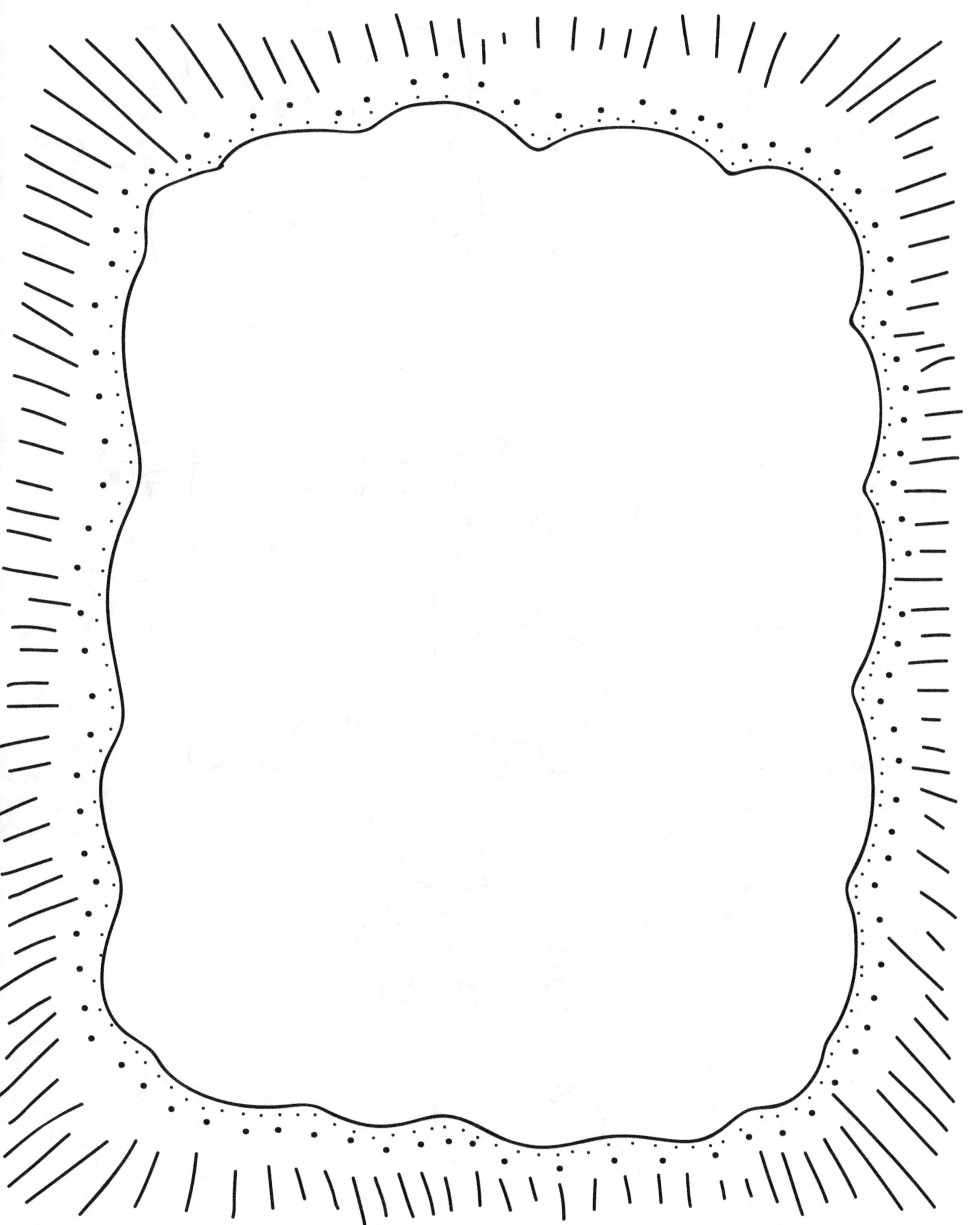

How to Draw a Giraffe

Now You Try!

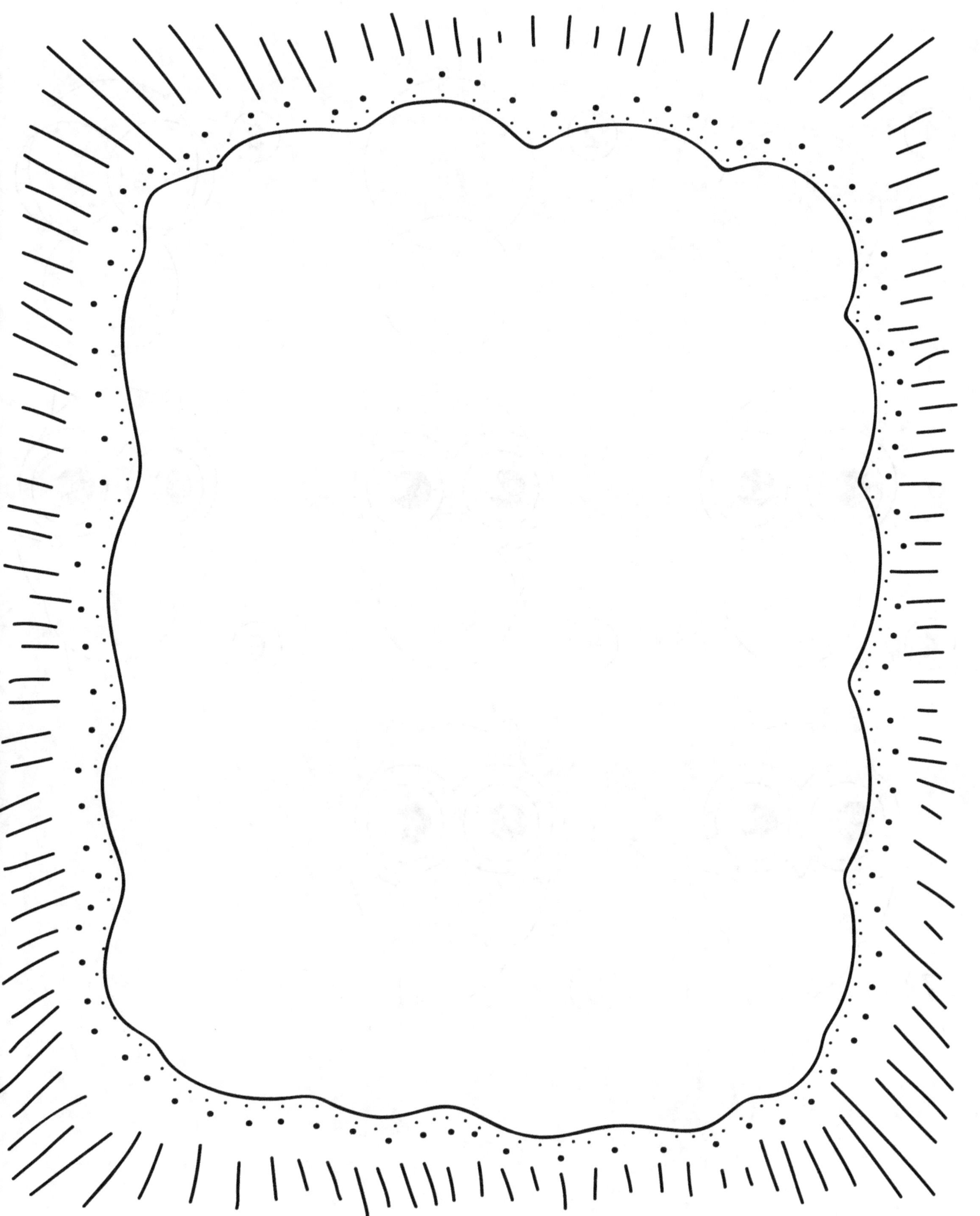

How to Draw an Owl

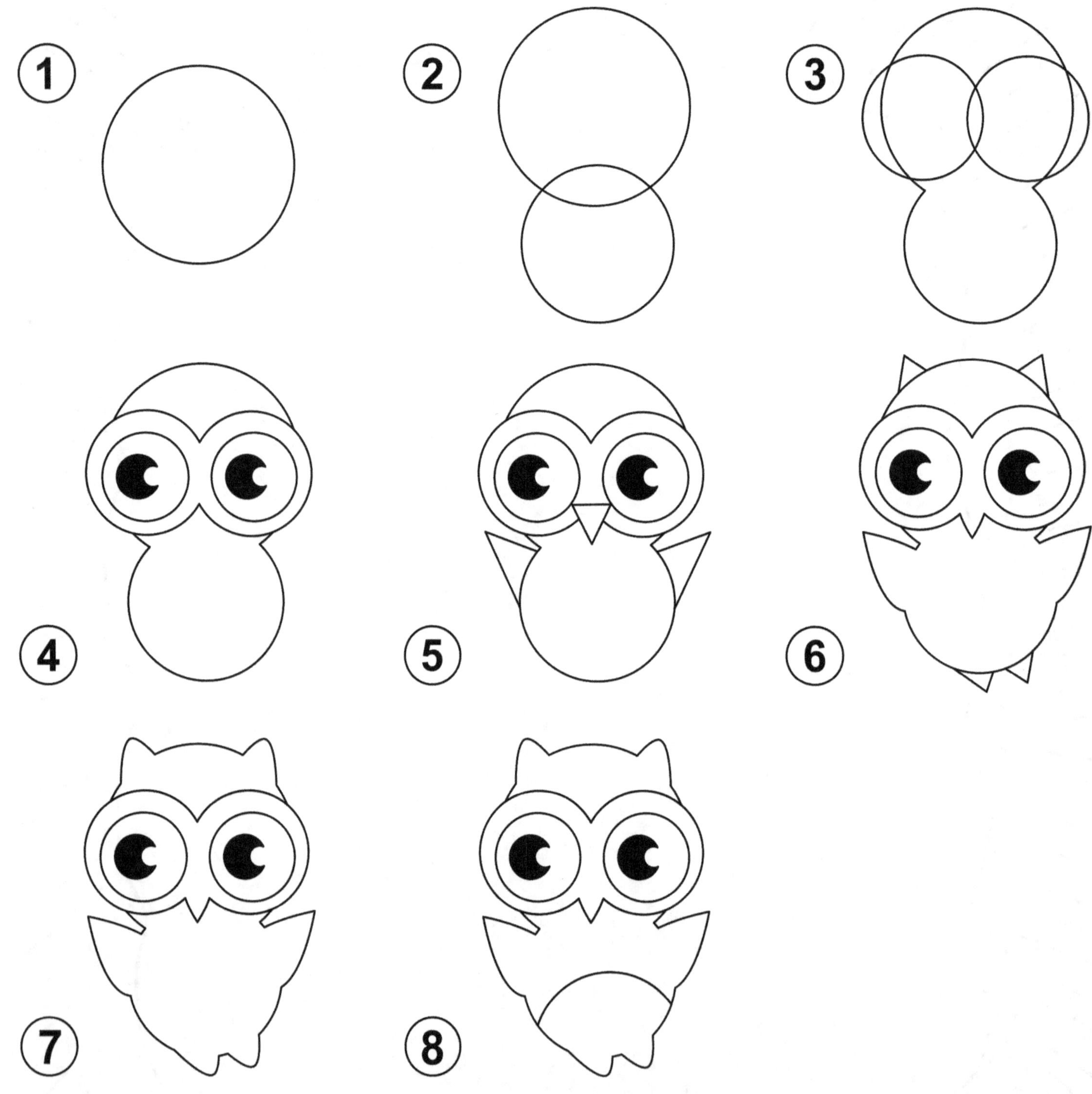

Now You Try!

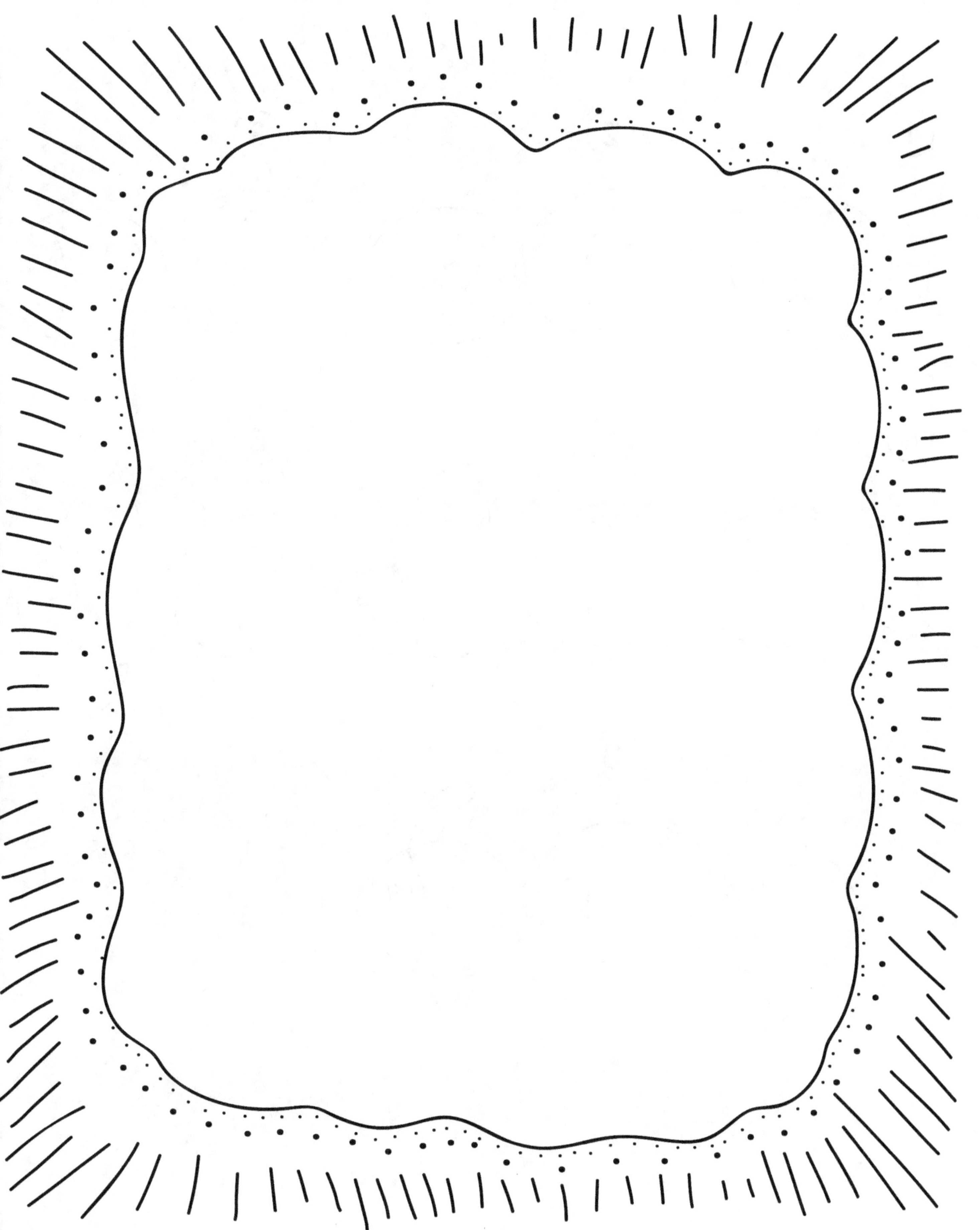

How to Draw a Fish

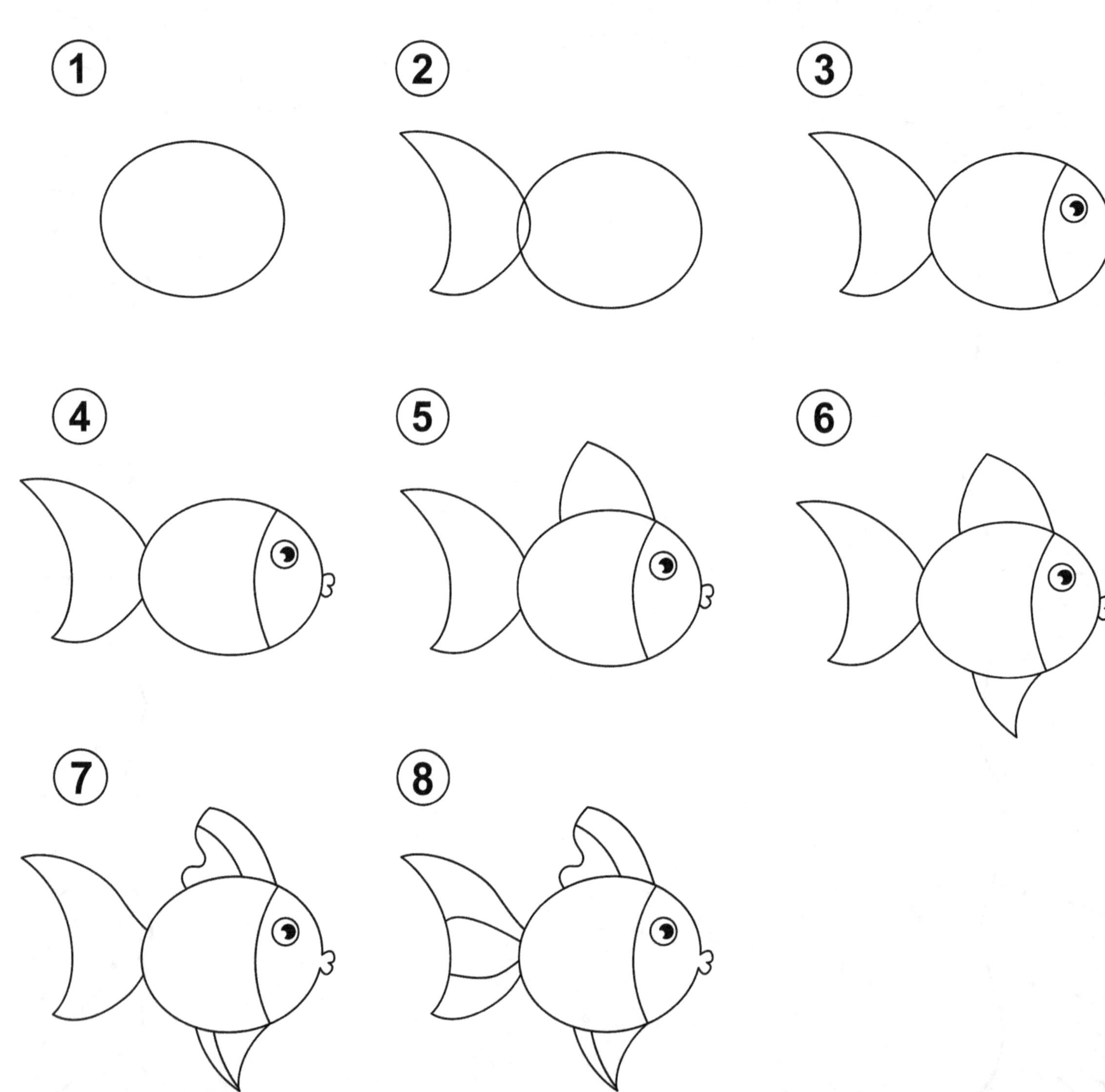

Now You Try!

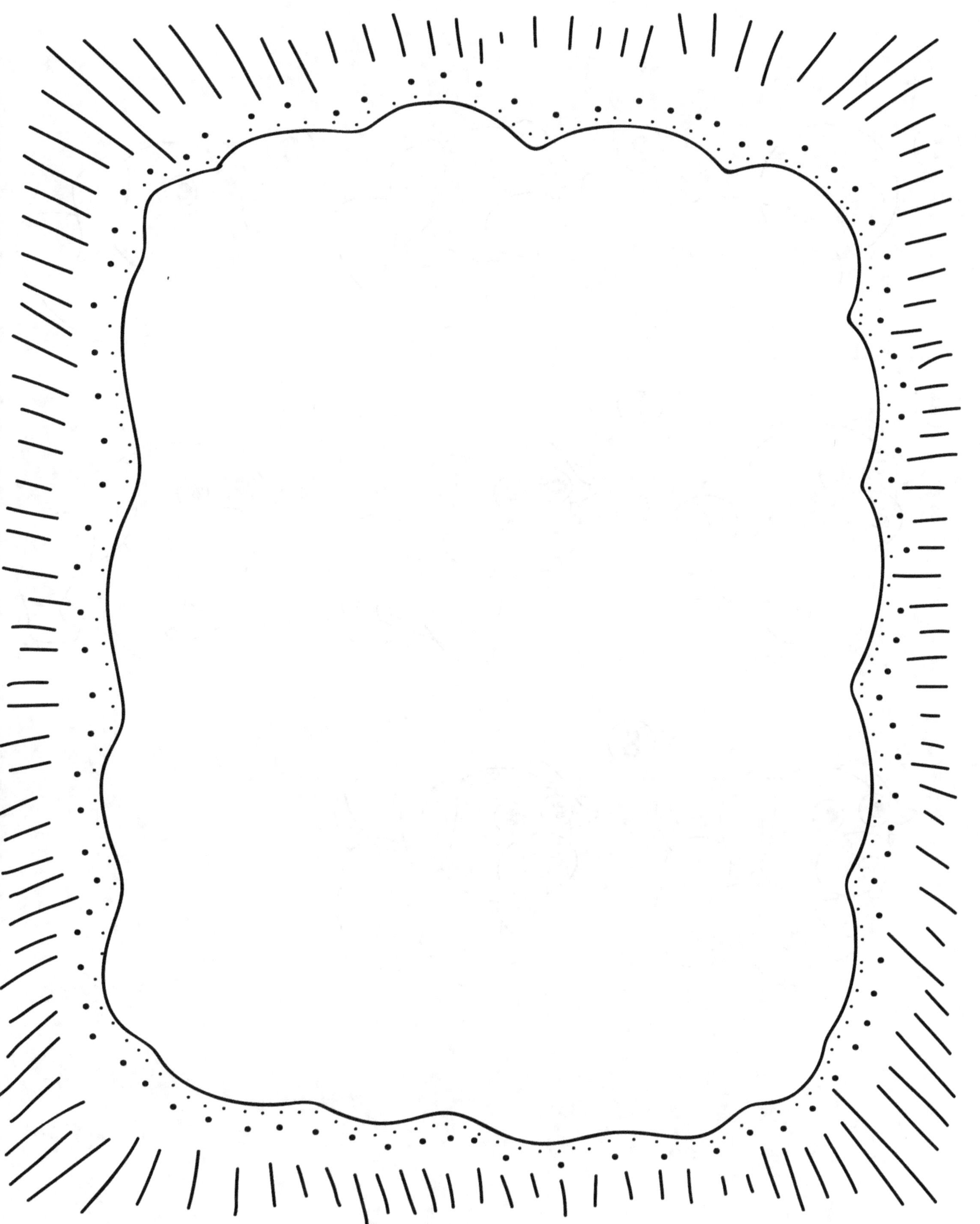

How to Draw a Dog

Now You Try!

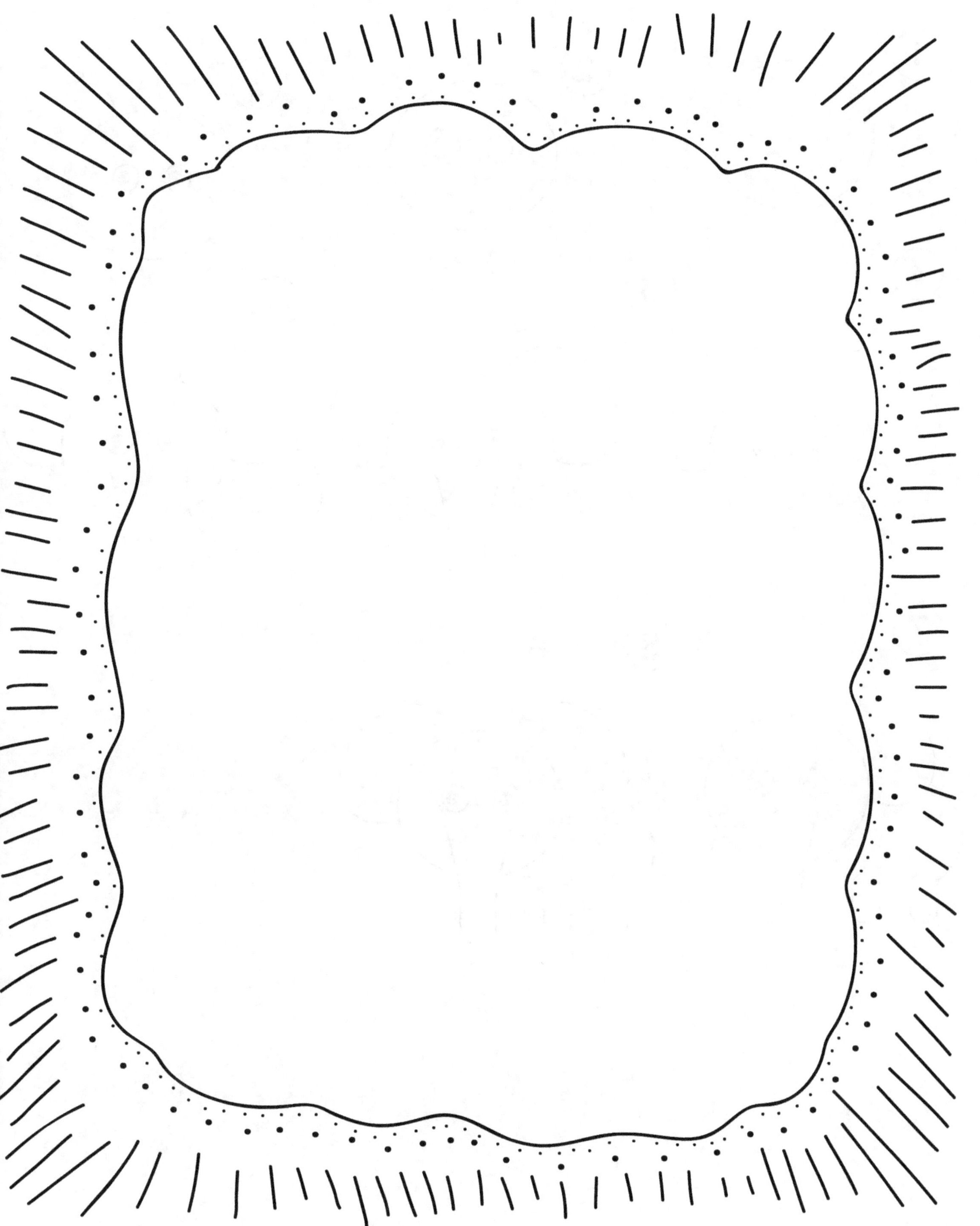

How to Draw an Elephant

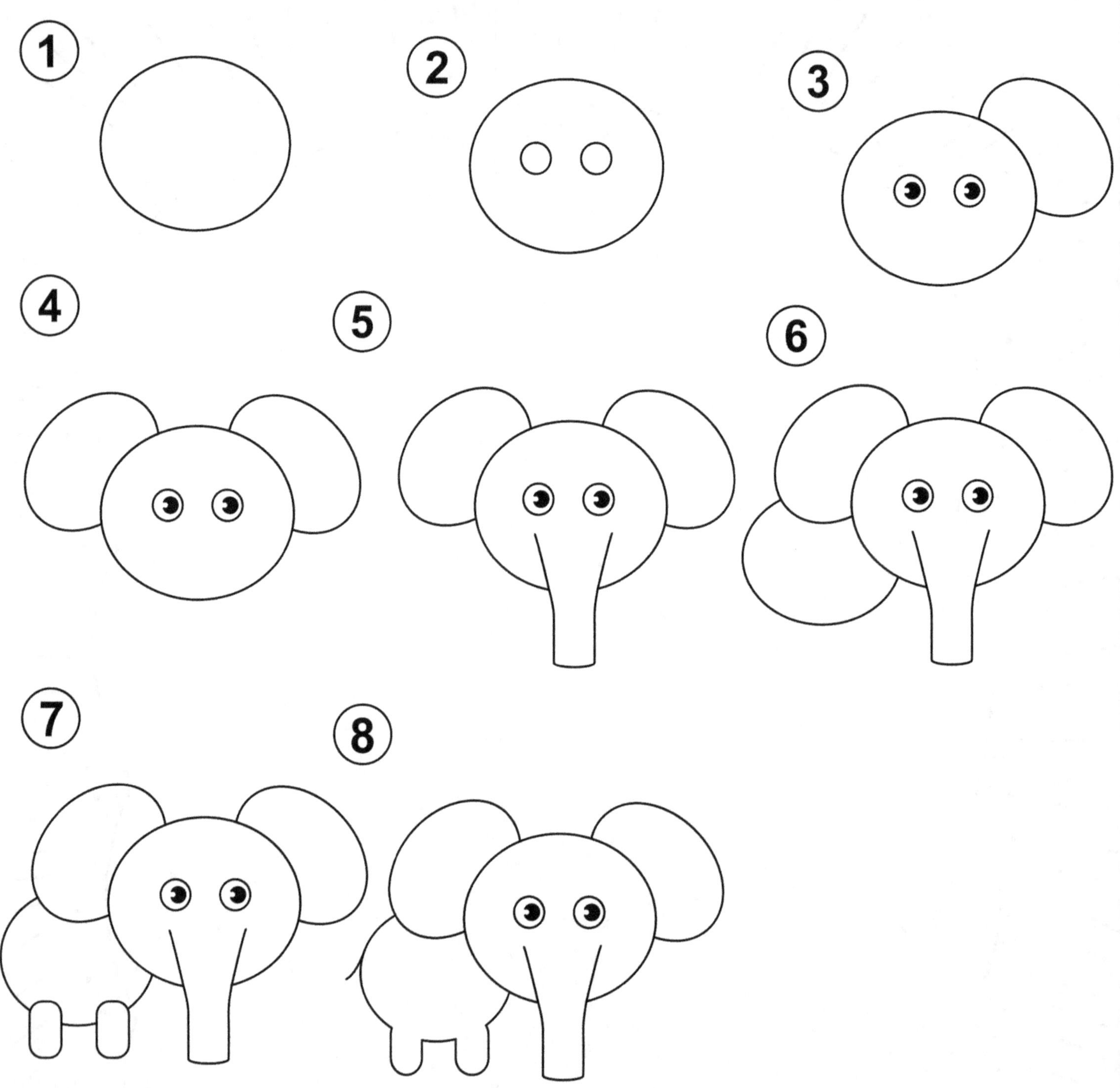

NOW YOU TRY!

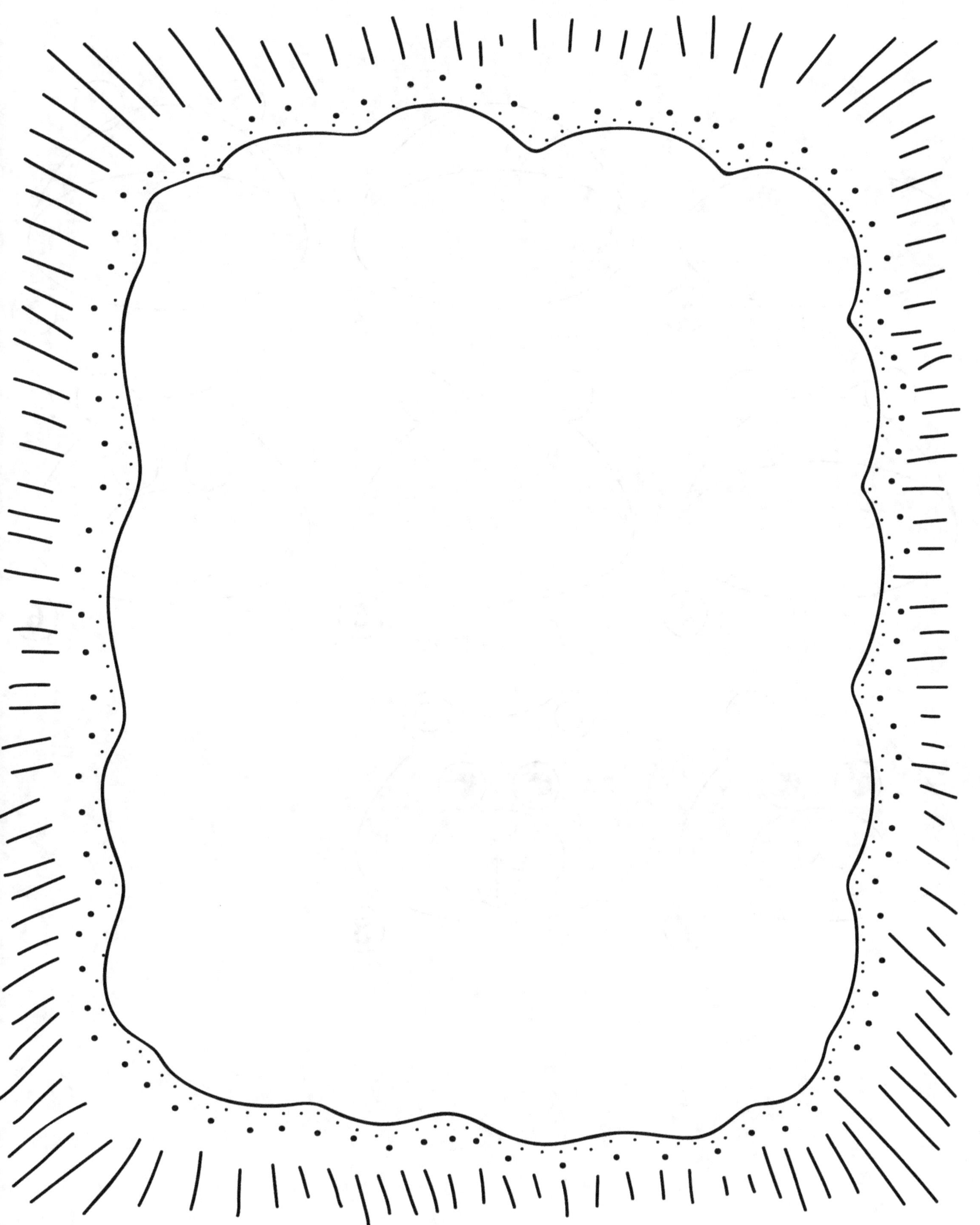

How to Draw a Beaver

Now You Try!

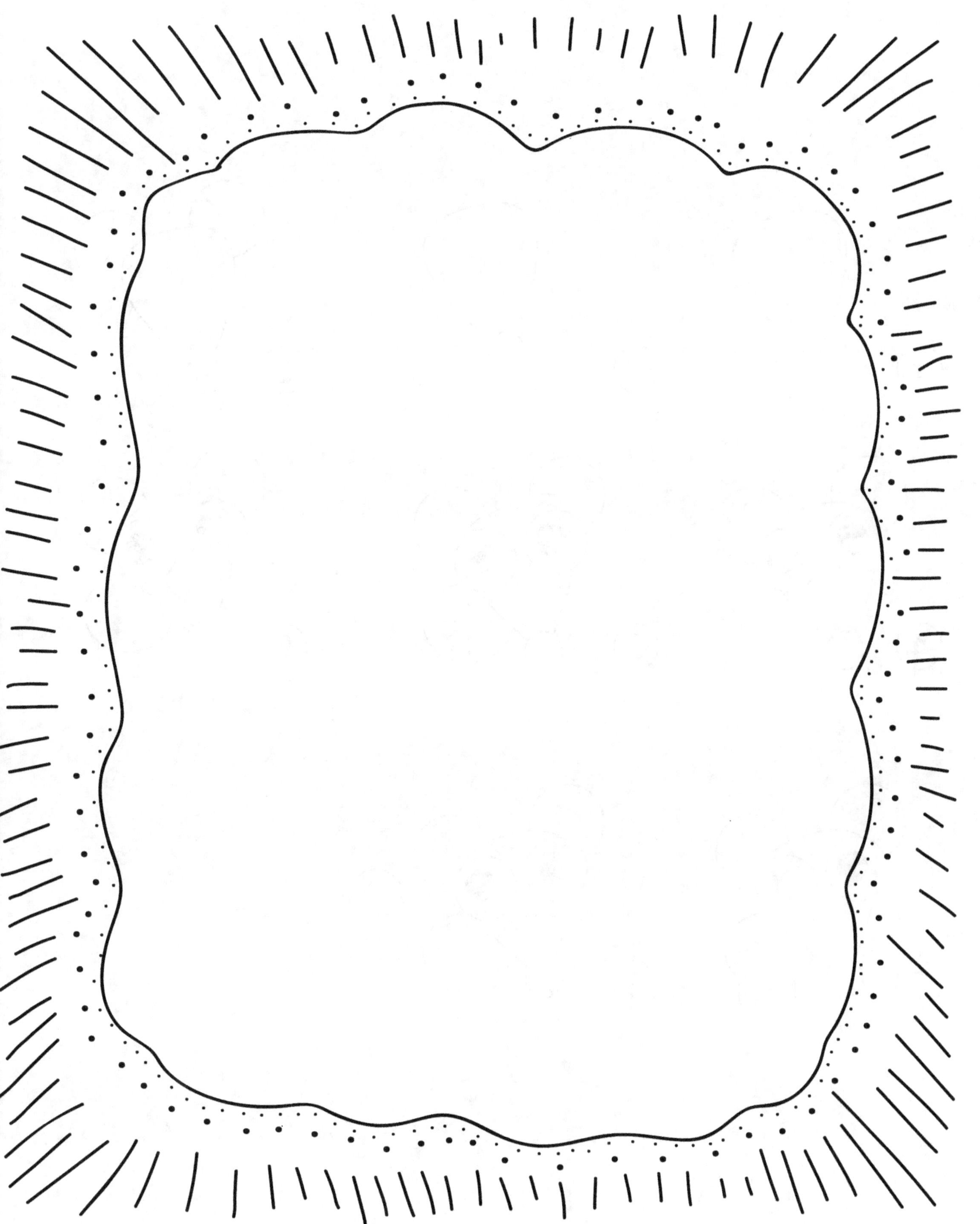

How to Draw a Mouse

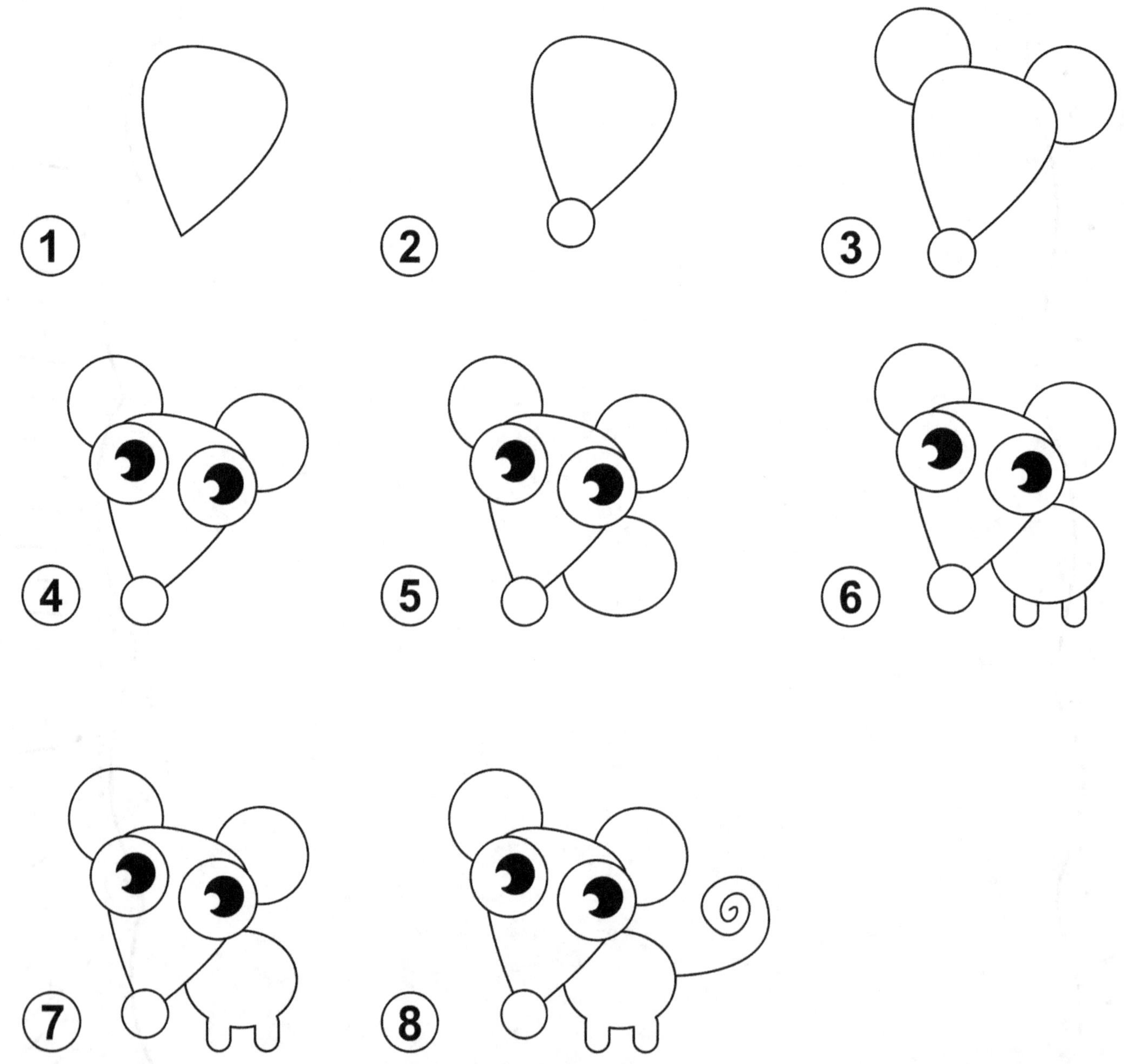

NOW YOU TRY!

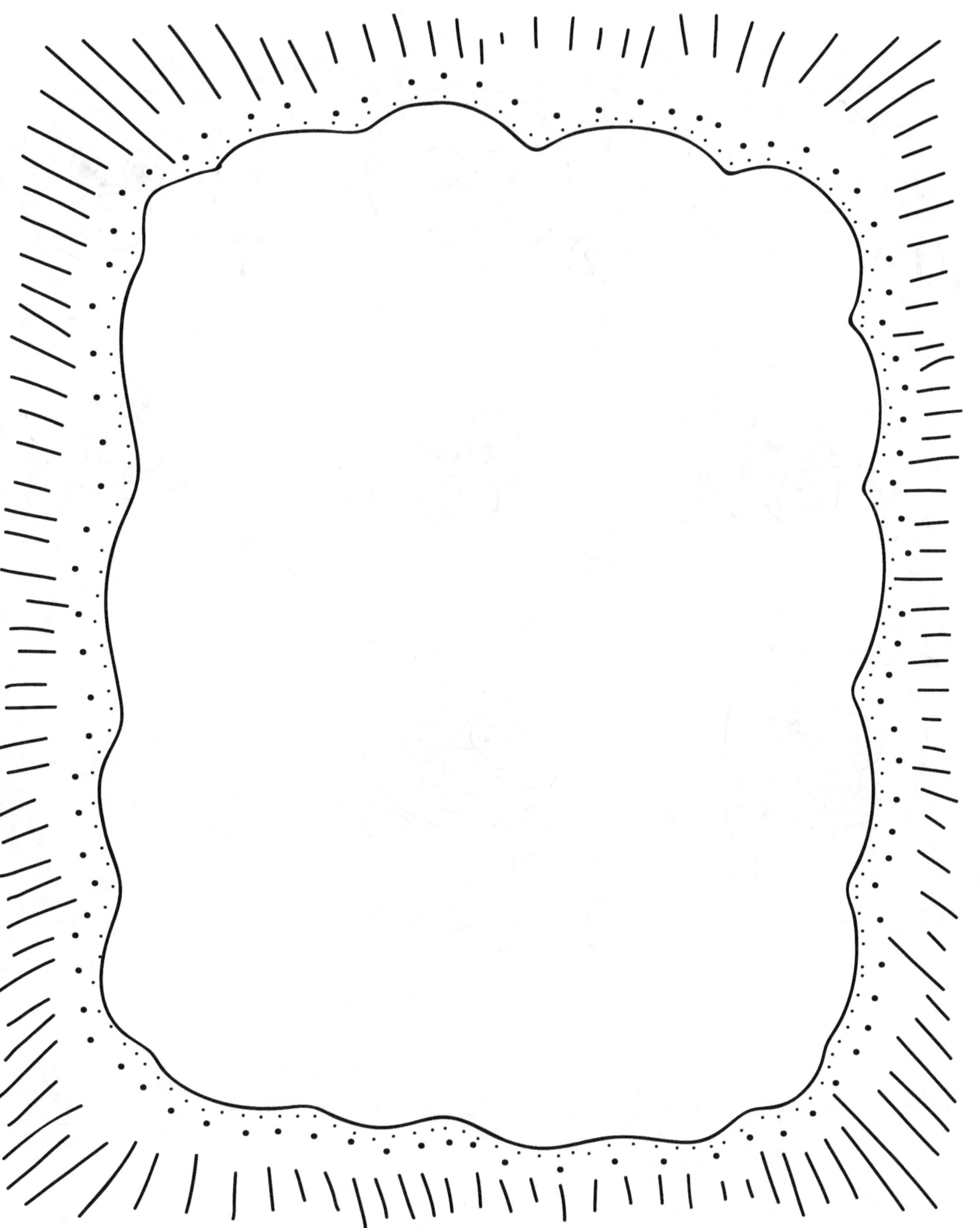

How to Draw a Bear

Now You Try!

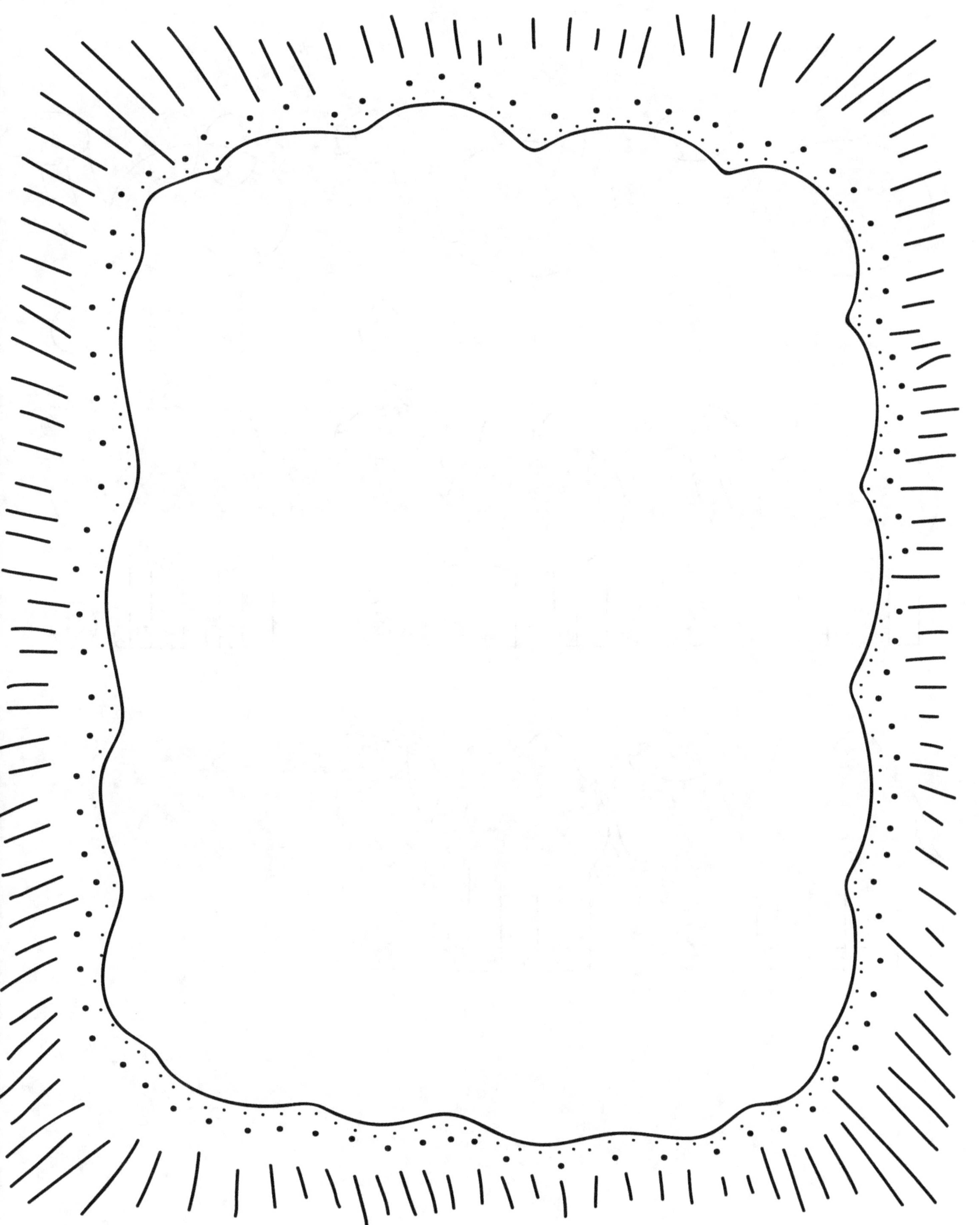

How to Draw a Camel

NOW YOU TRY!

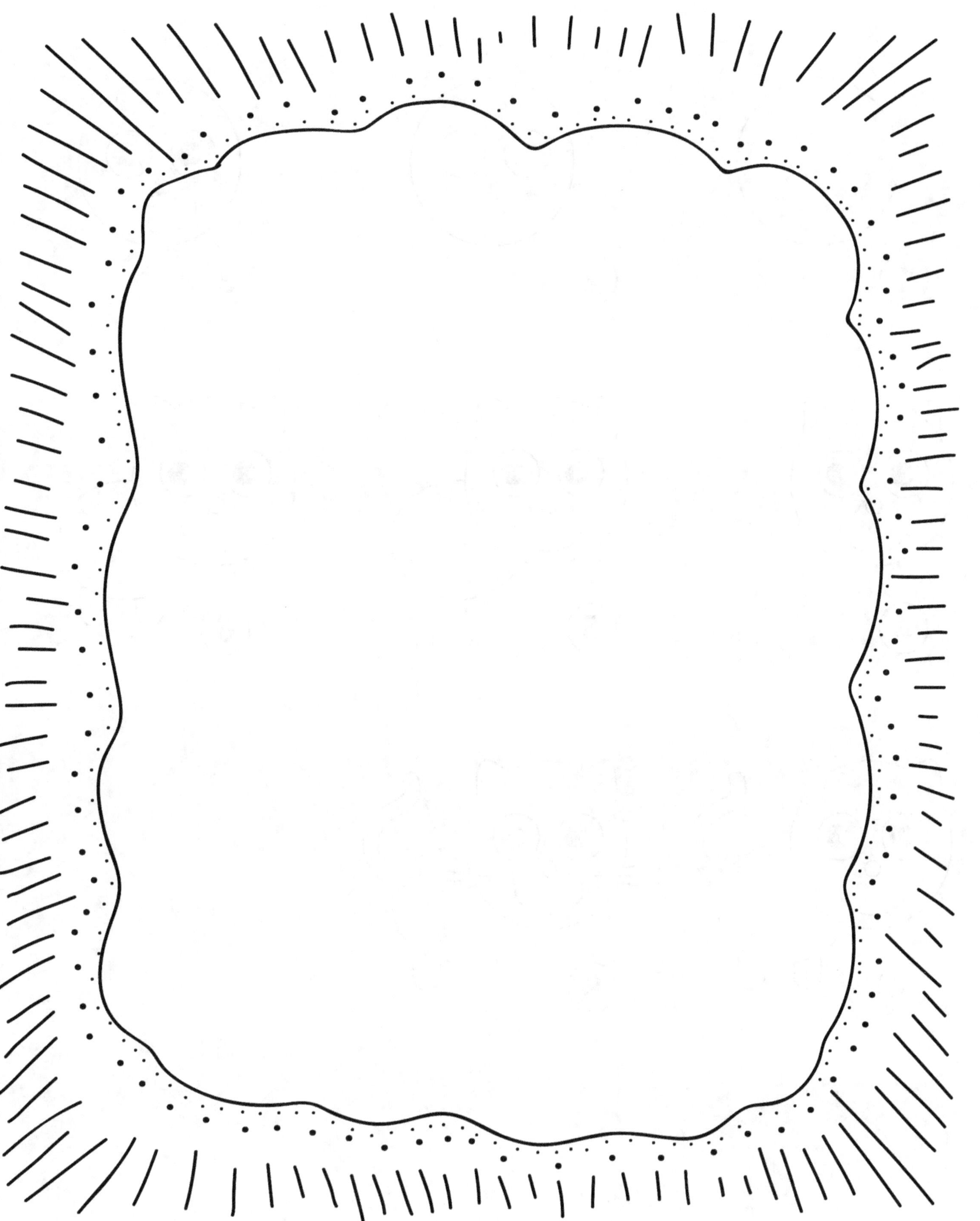

How to Draw a Cat

Now You Try!

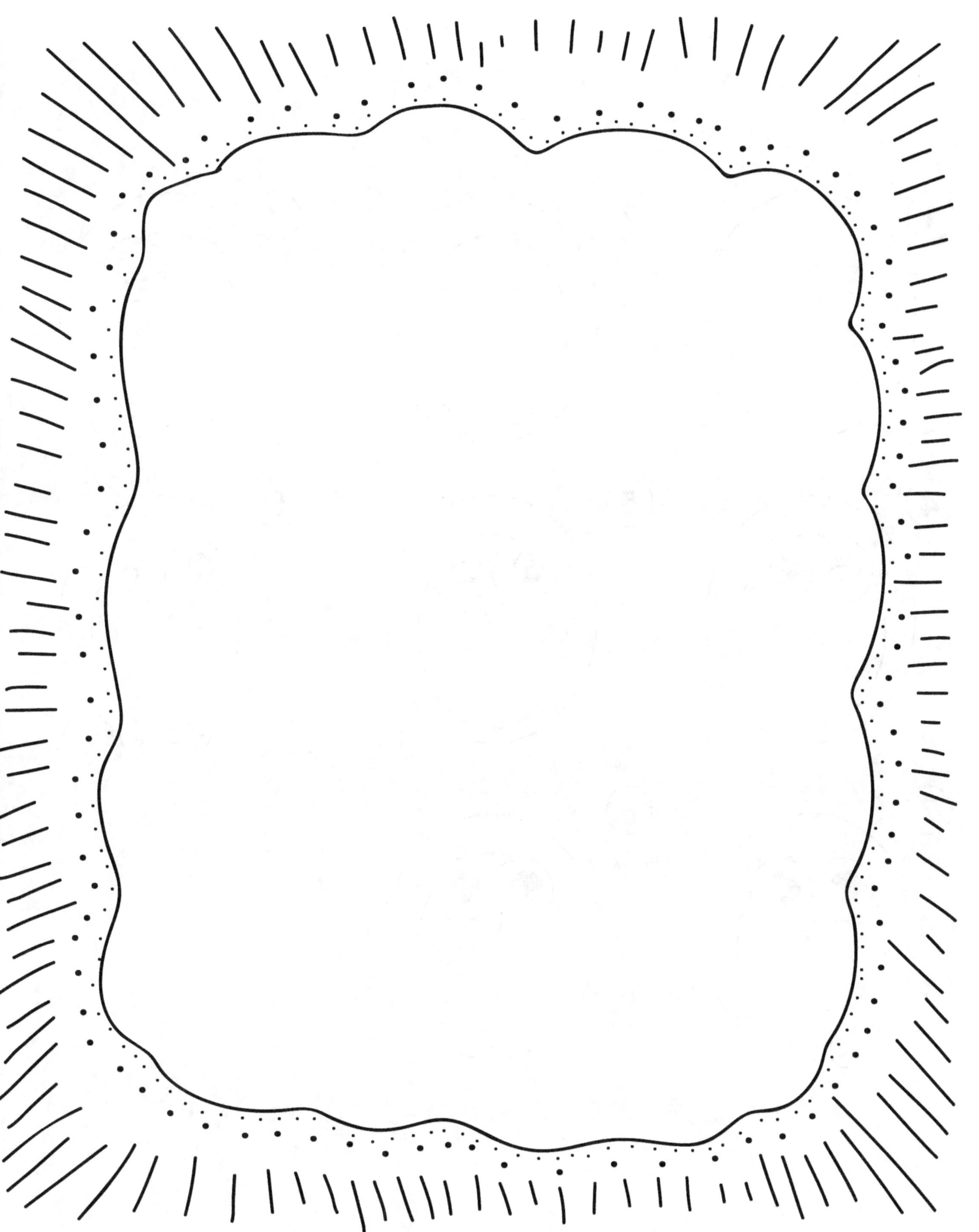

How to Draw a Penguin

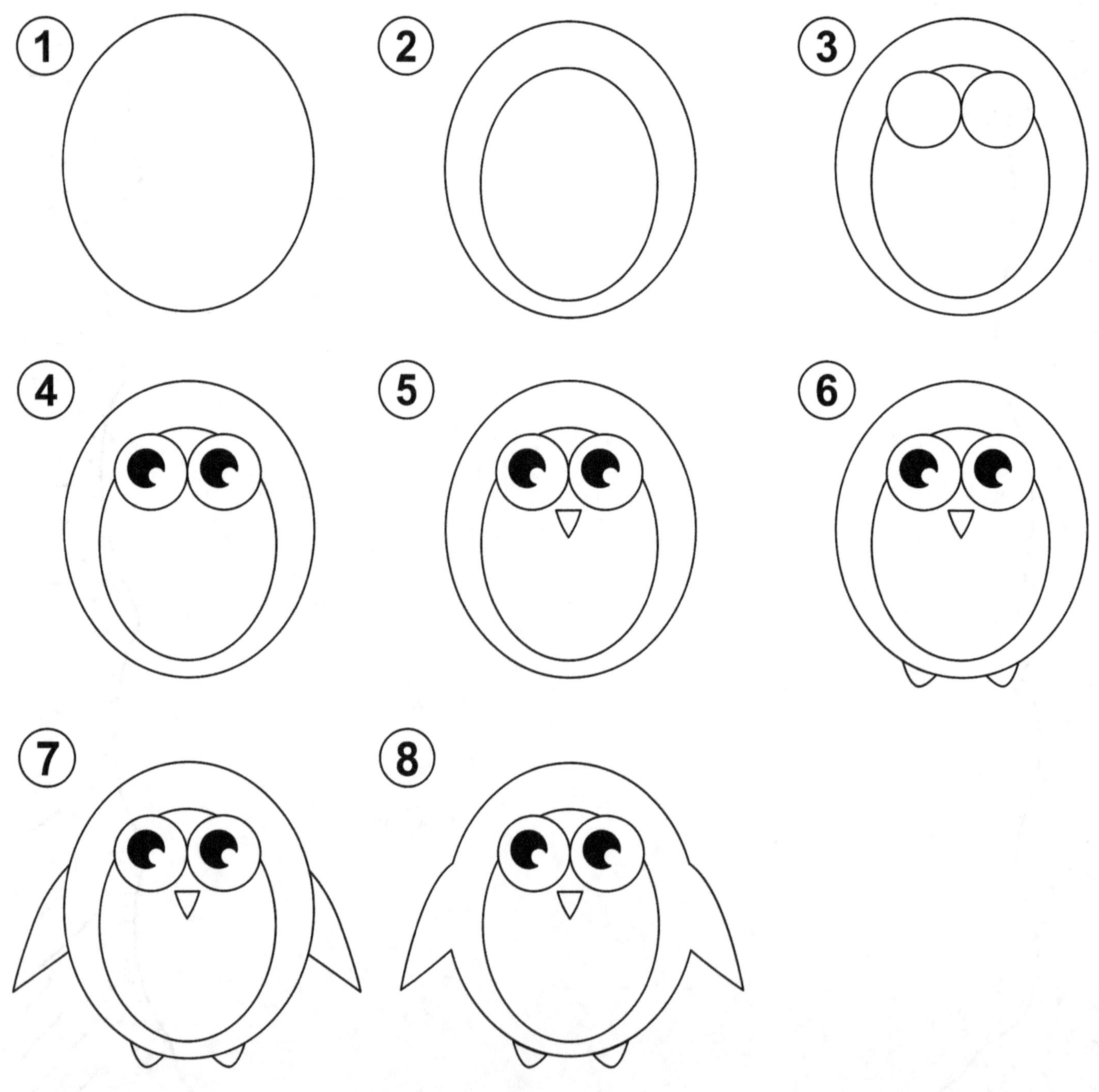

Now You Try!

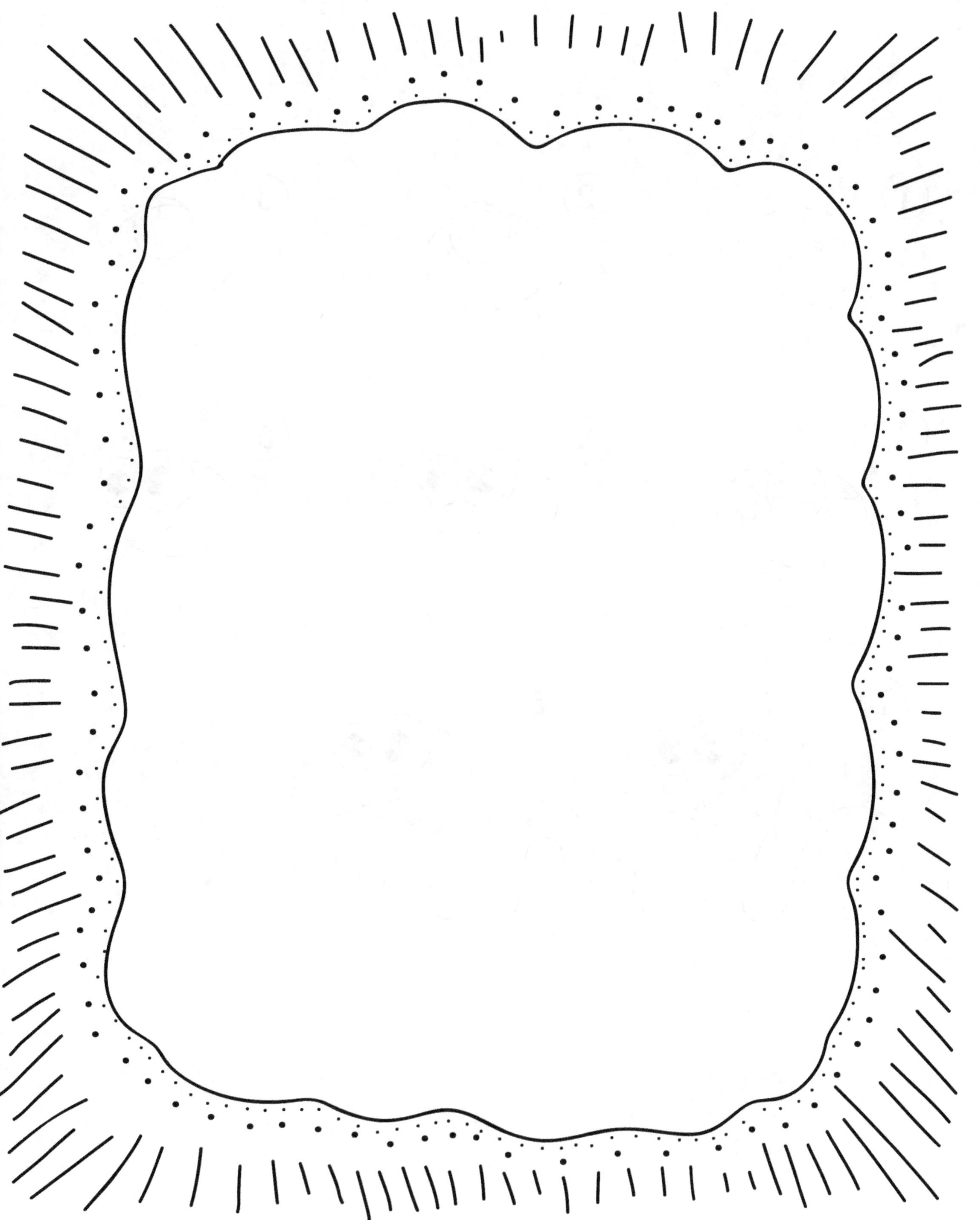

How to Draw a Snake

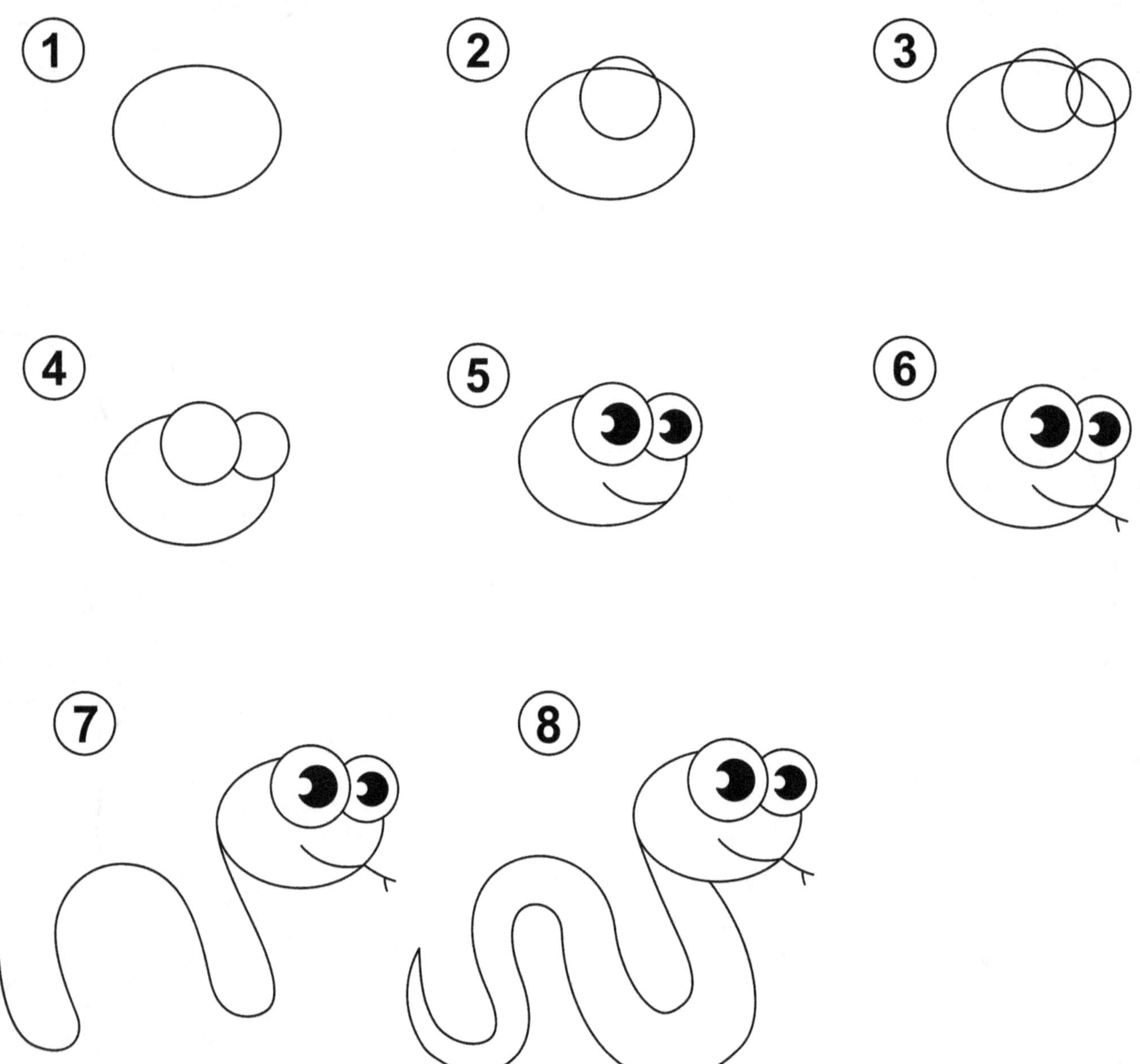

NOW YOU TRY!

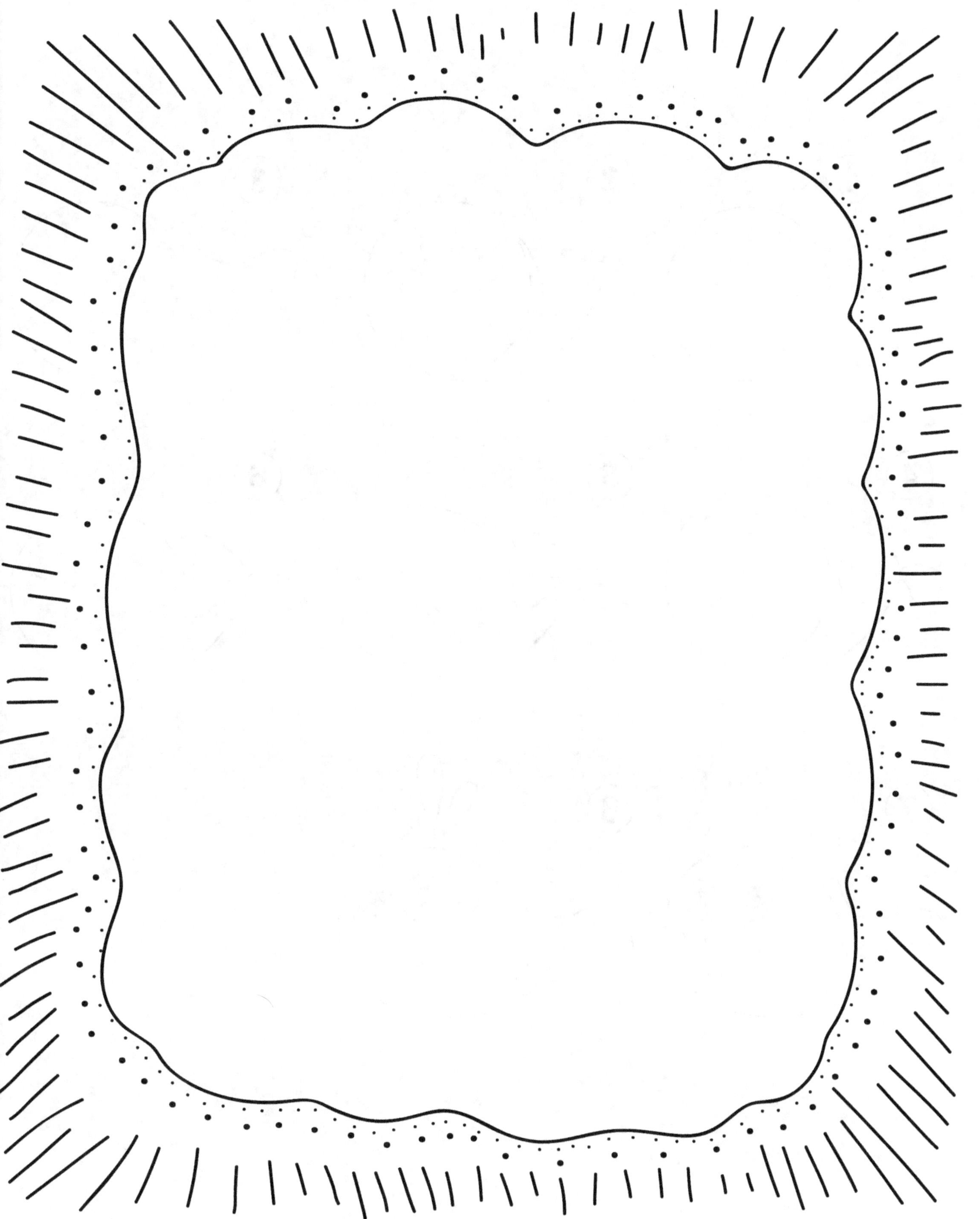

How to Draw a Whale

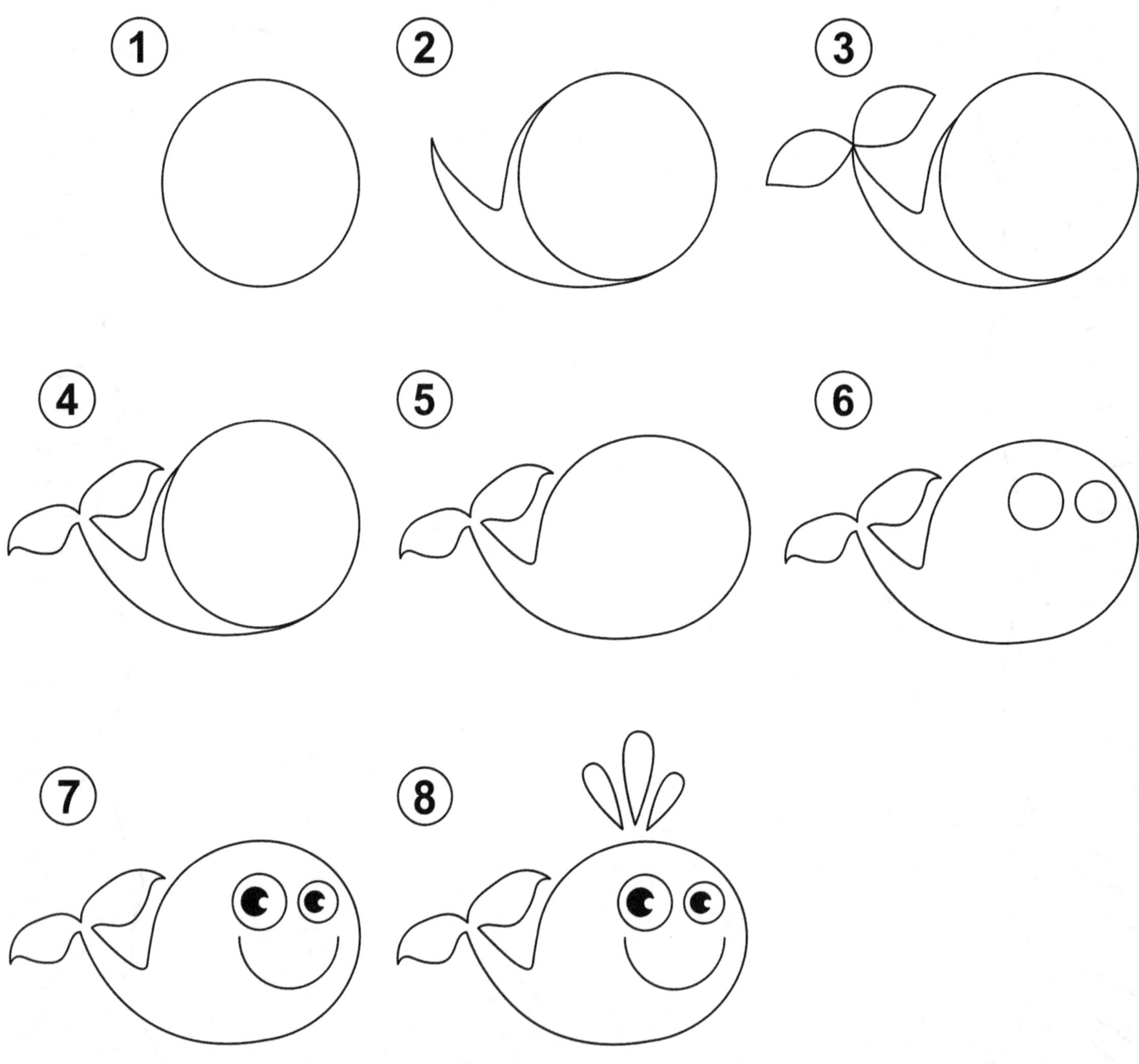

Now You Try!

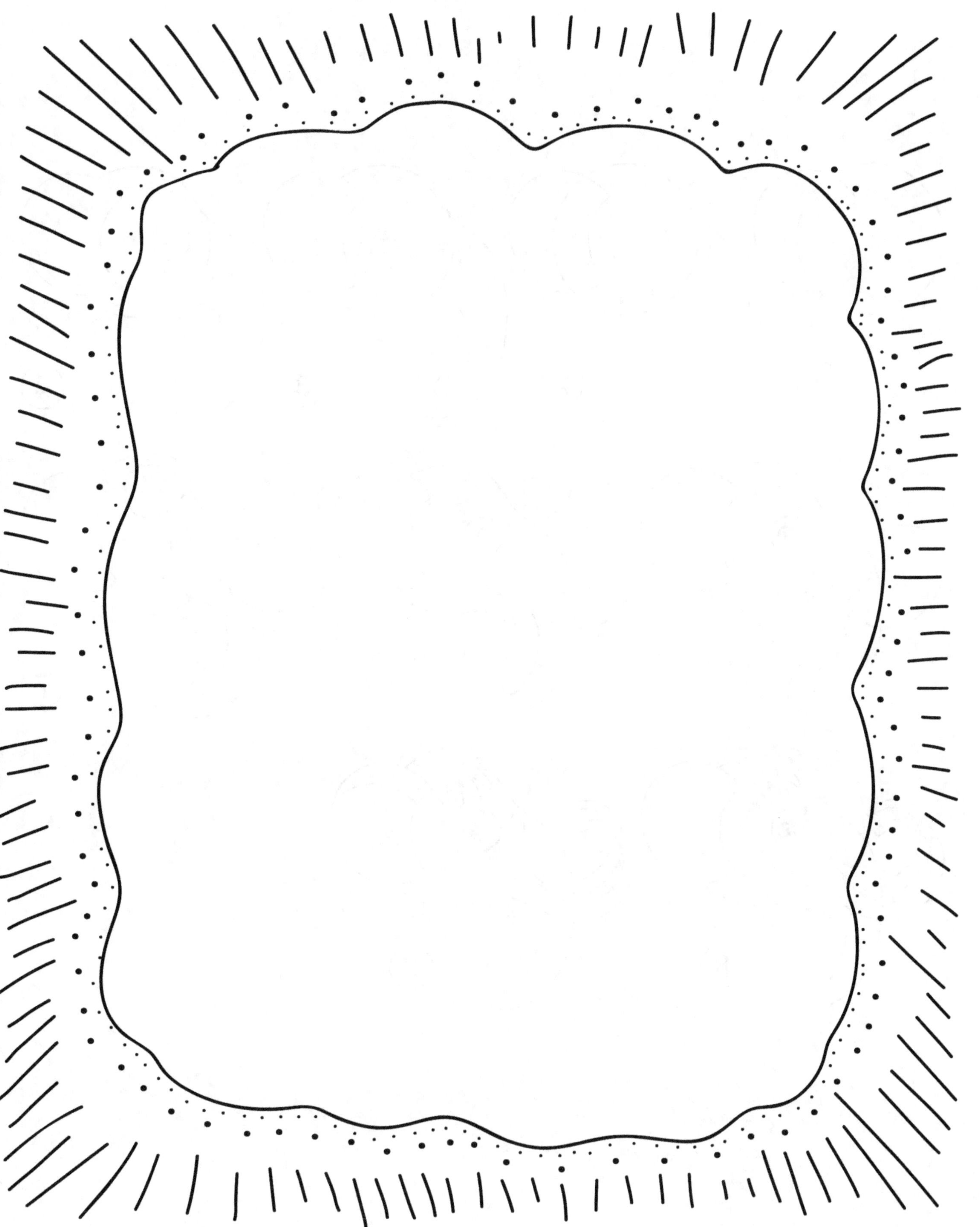

How to Draw a Mammoth

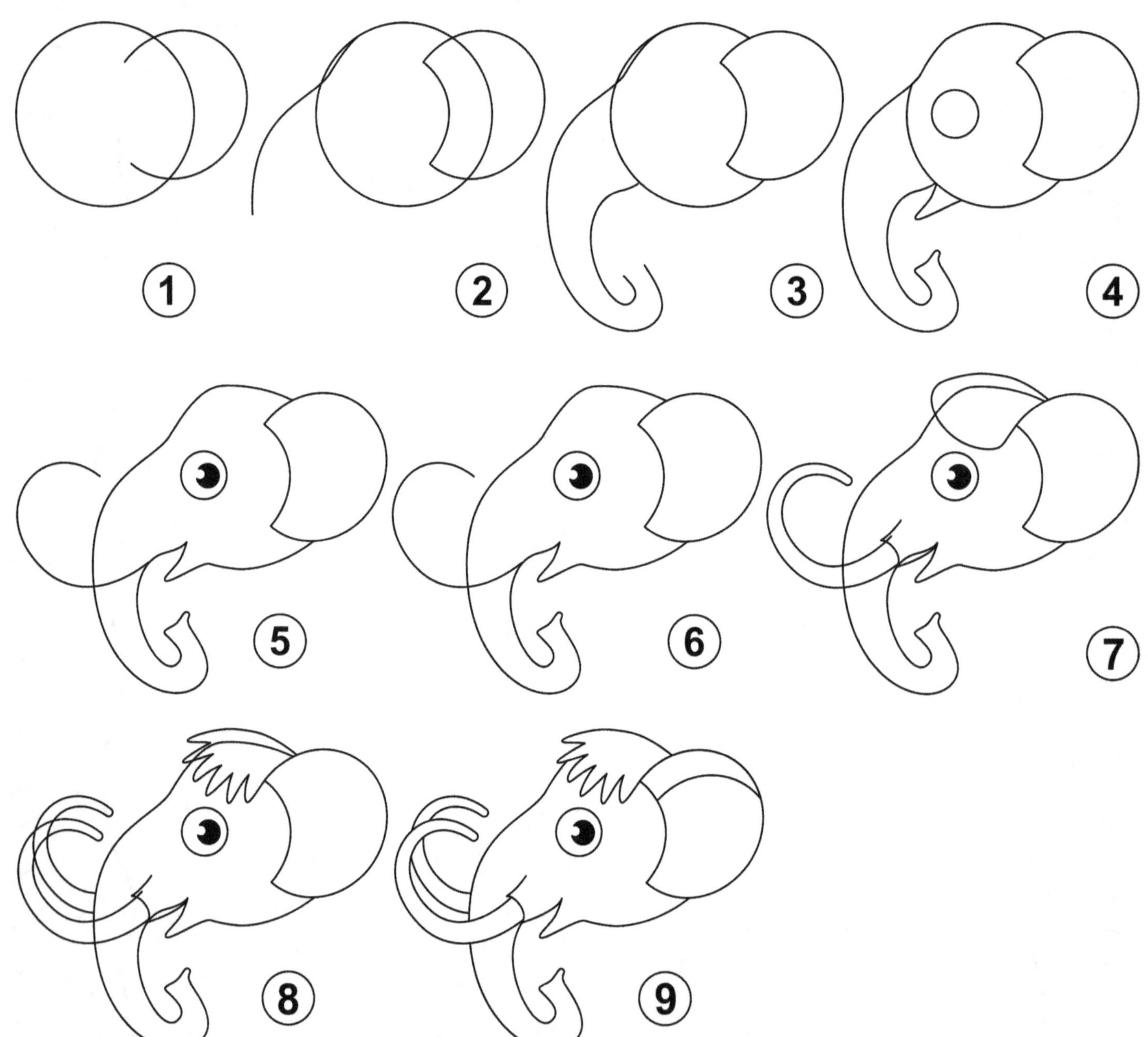

Now You Try!

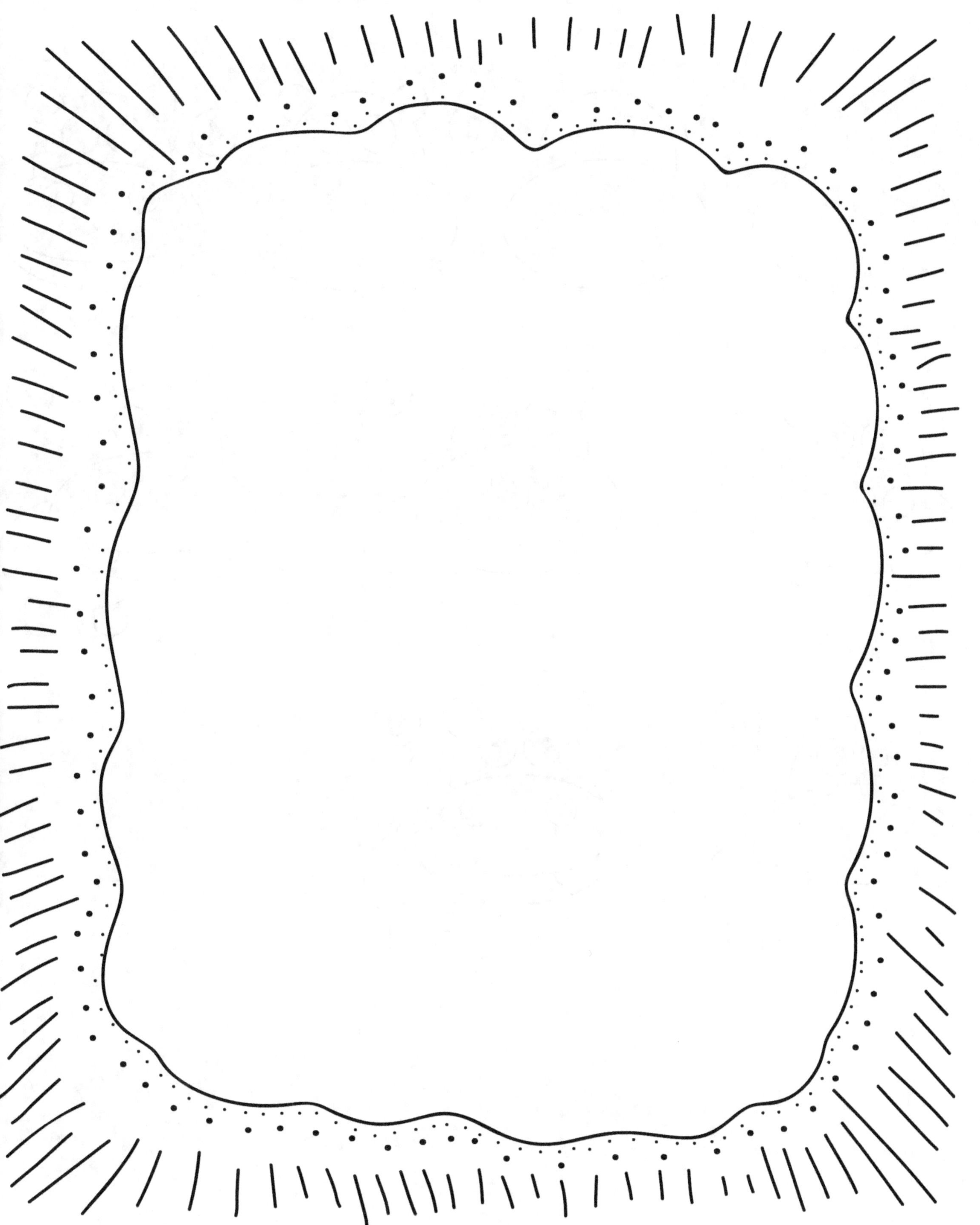

How to Draw a Hippo

Now You Try!

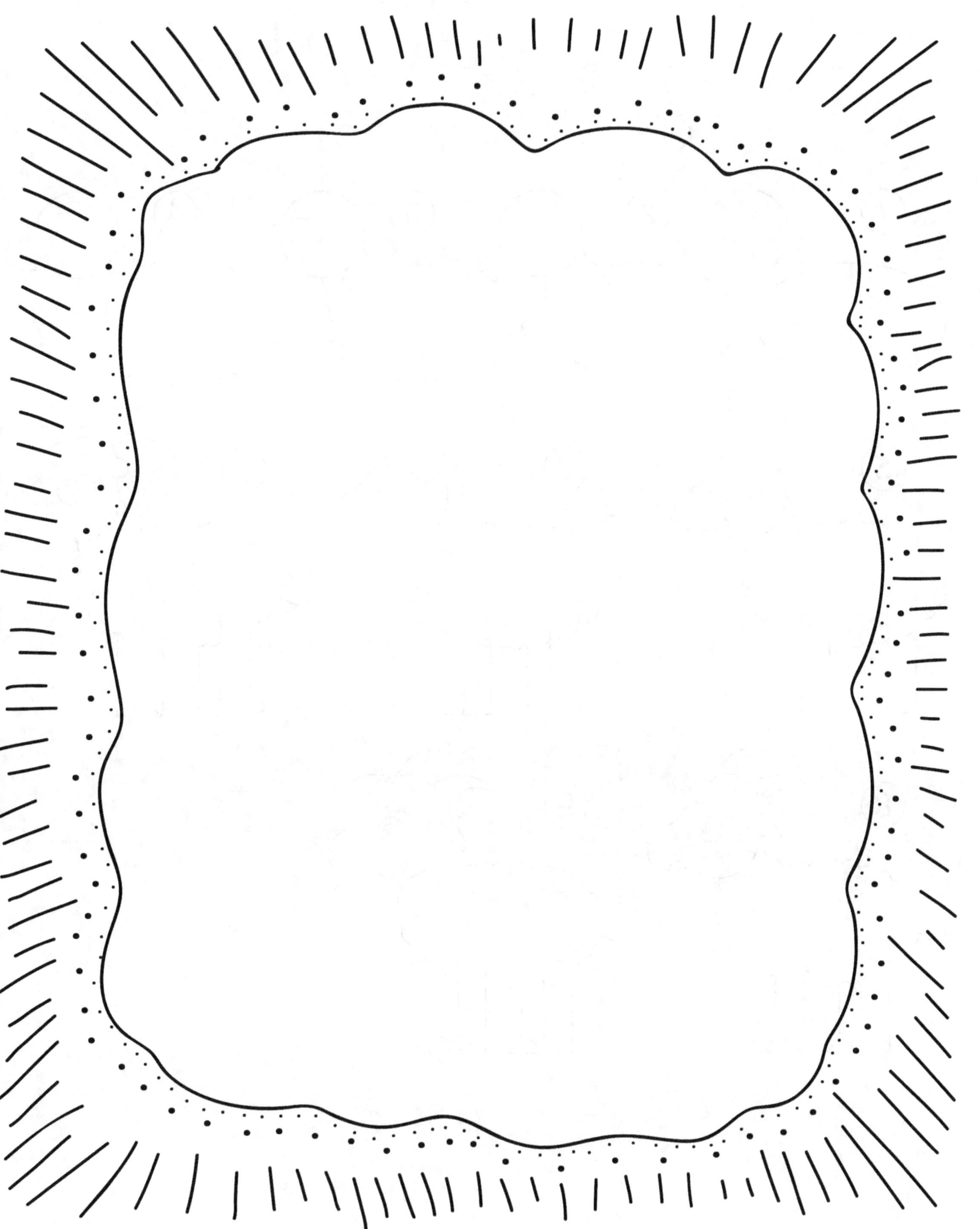

How to Draw a Goat

Now You Try!

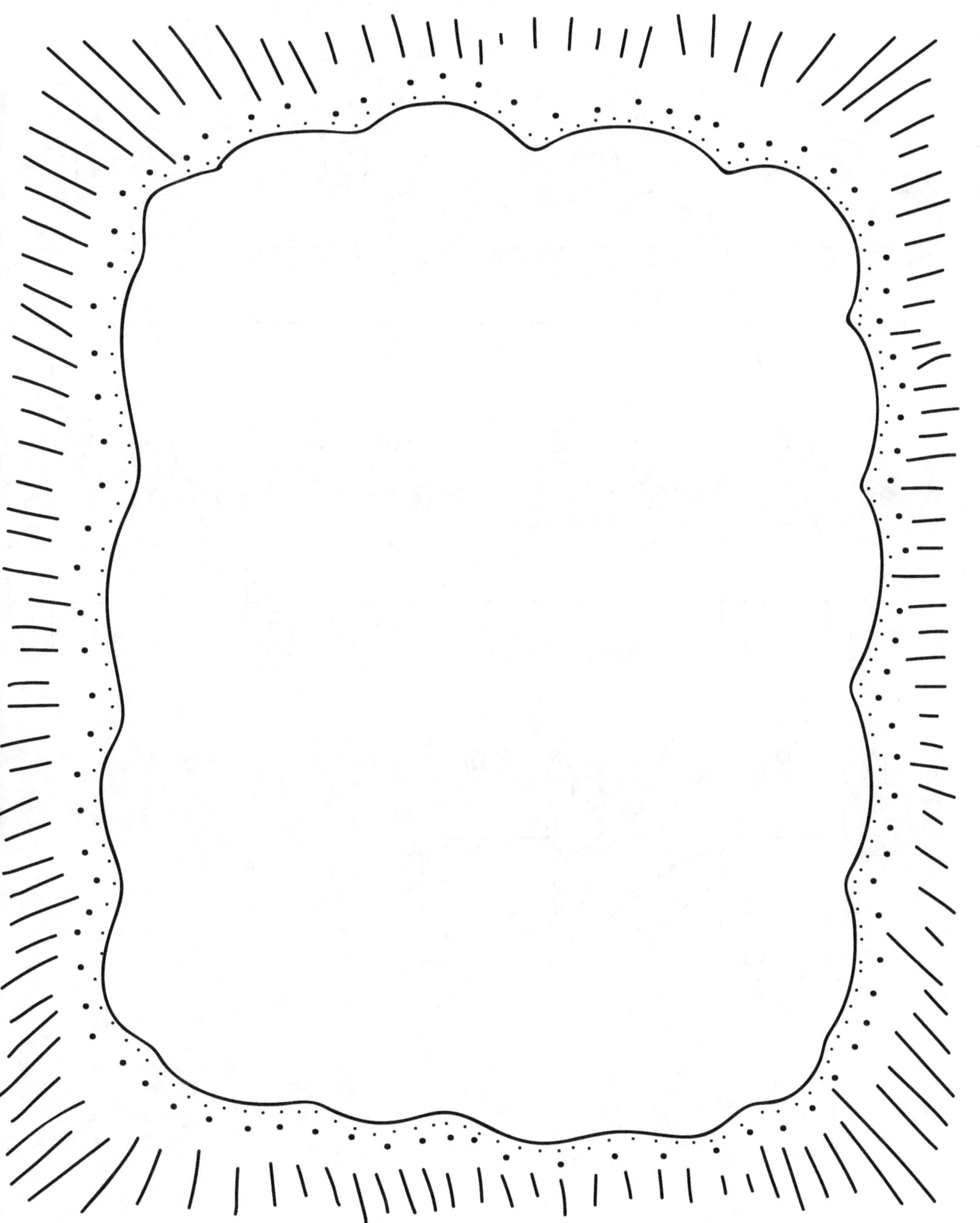

How to Draw a Fox

Now You Try!

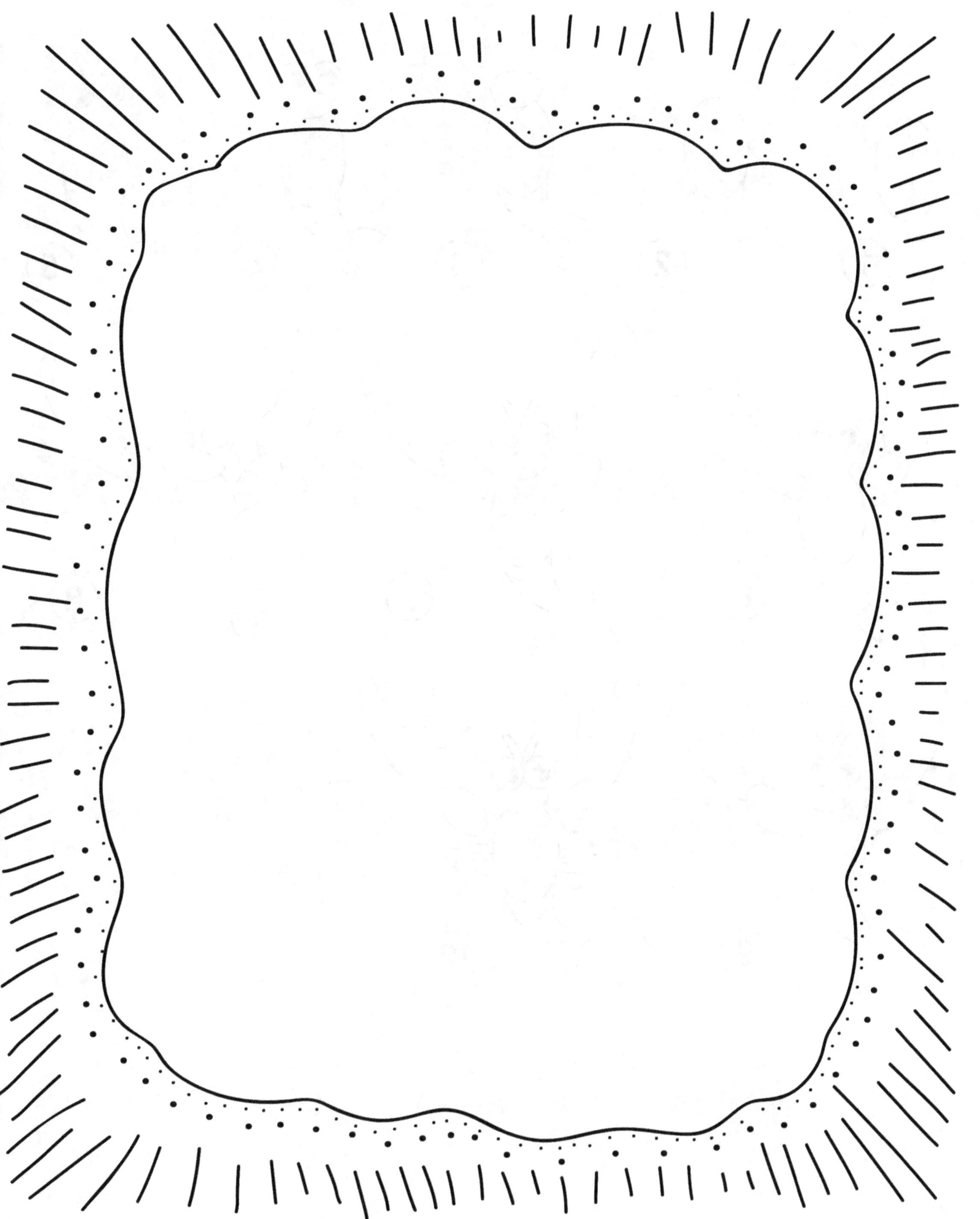

How to Draw a Lobster

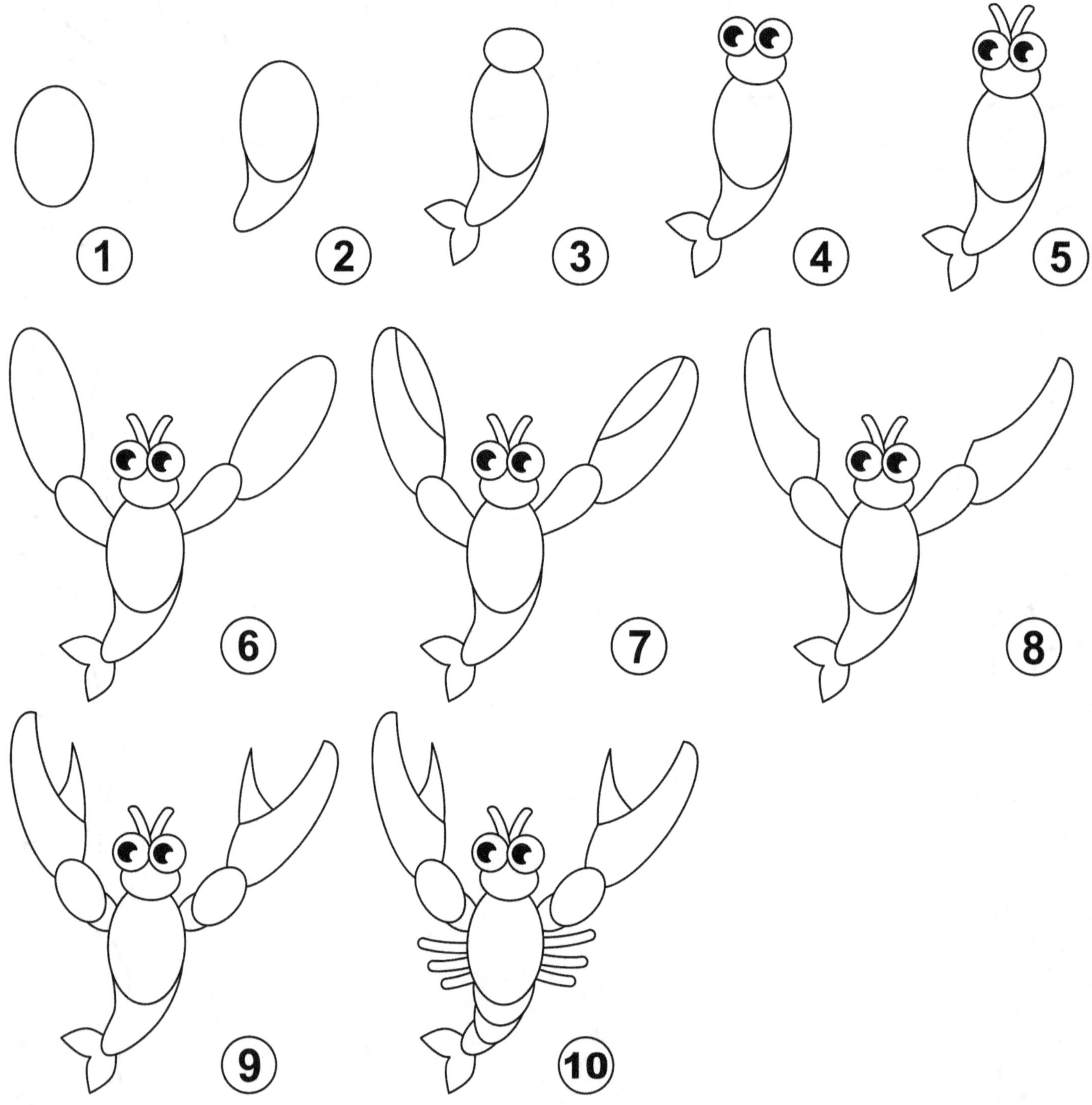

Now You Try!

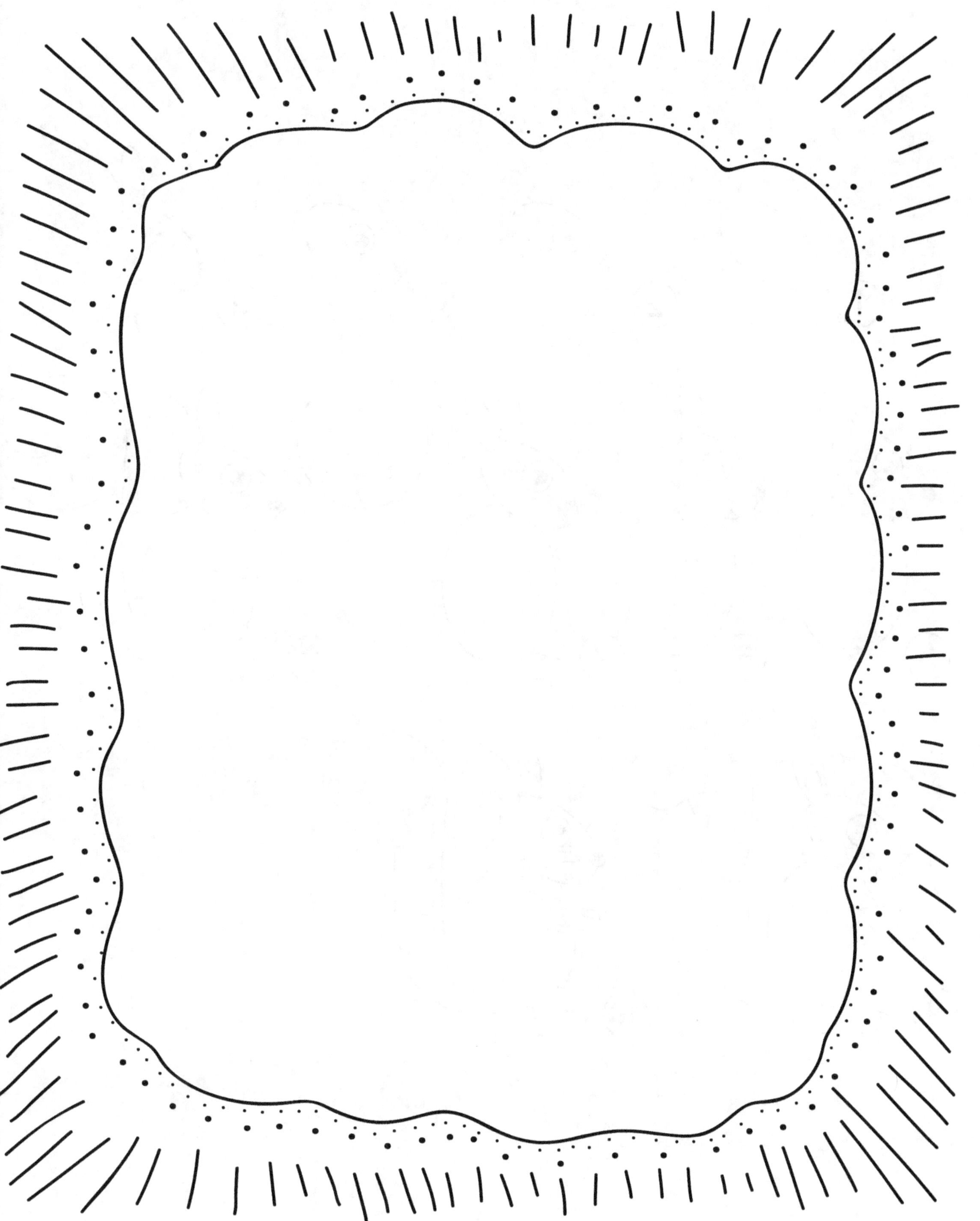

How to Draw a Squirrel

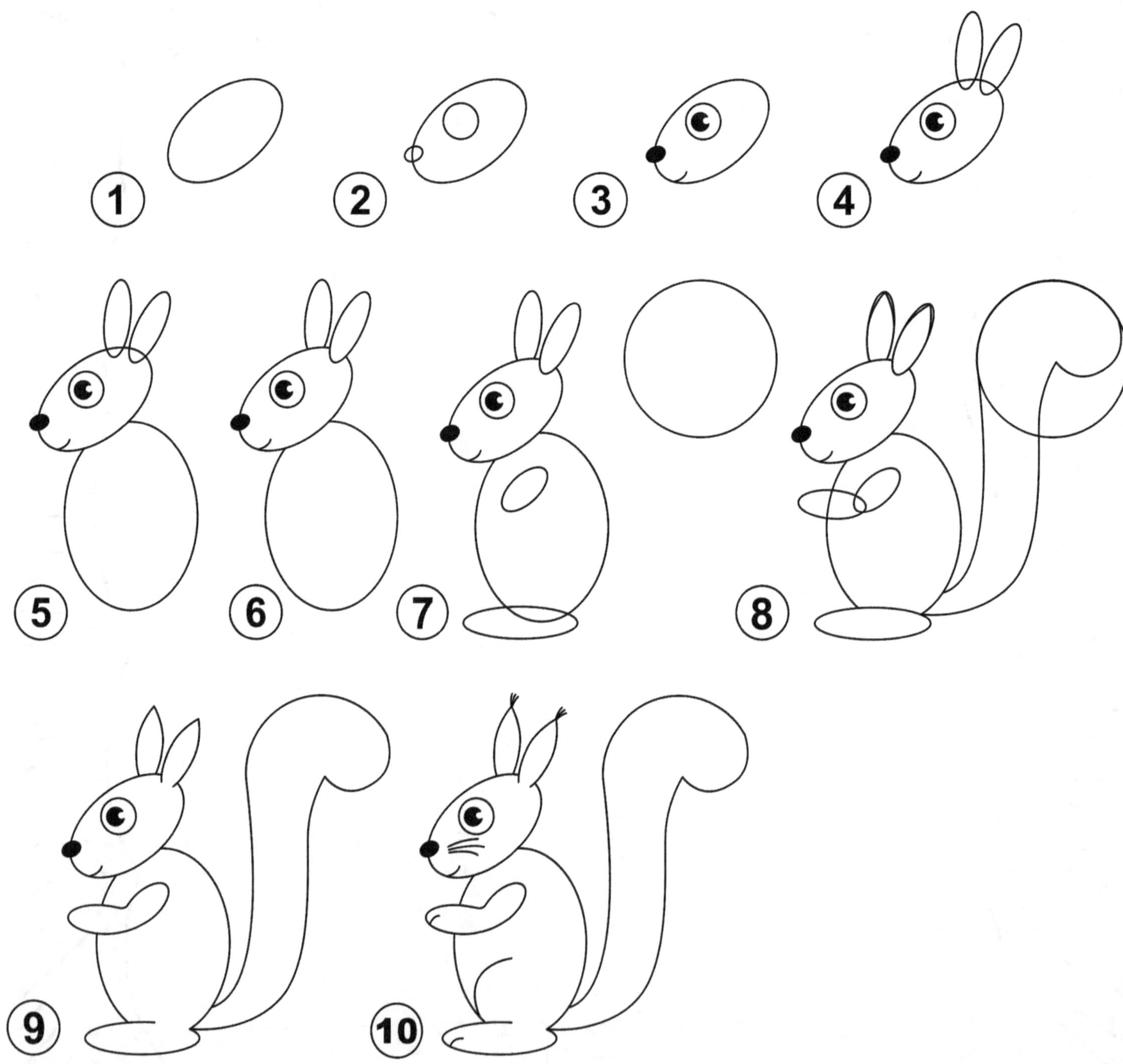

NOW YOU TRY!

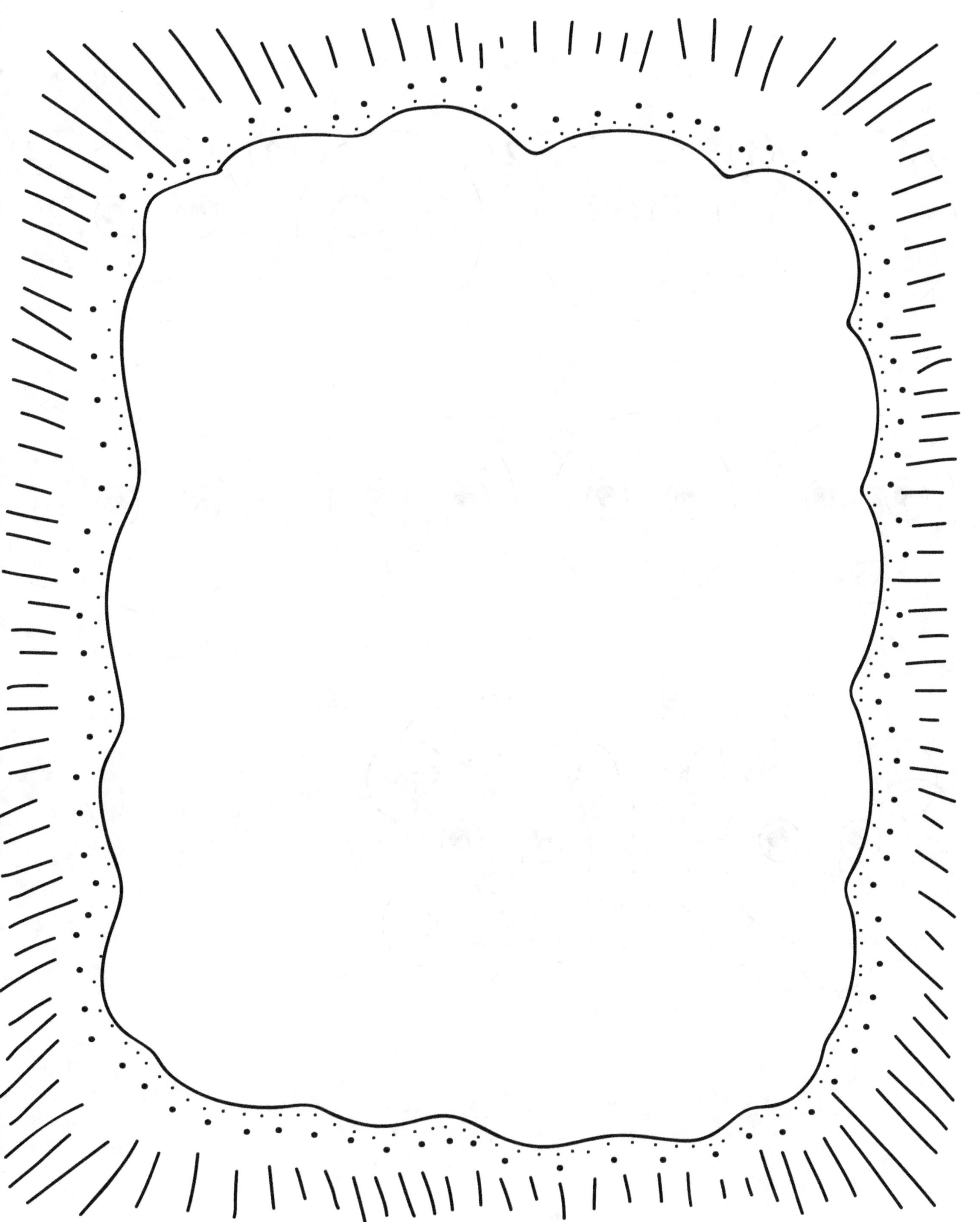

How to Draw a Lion

Now You Try!

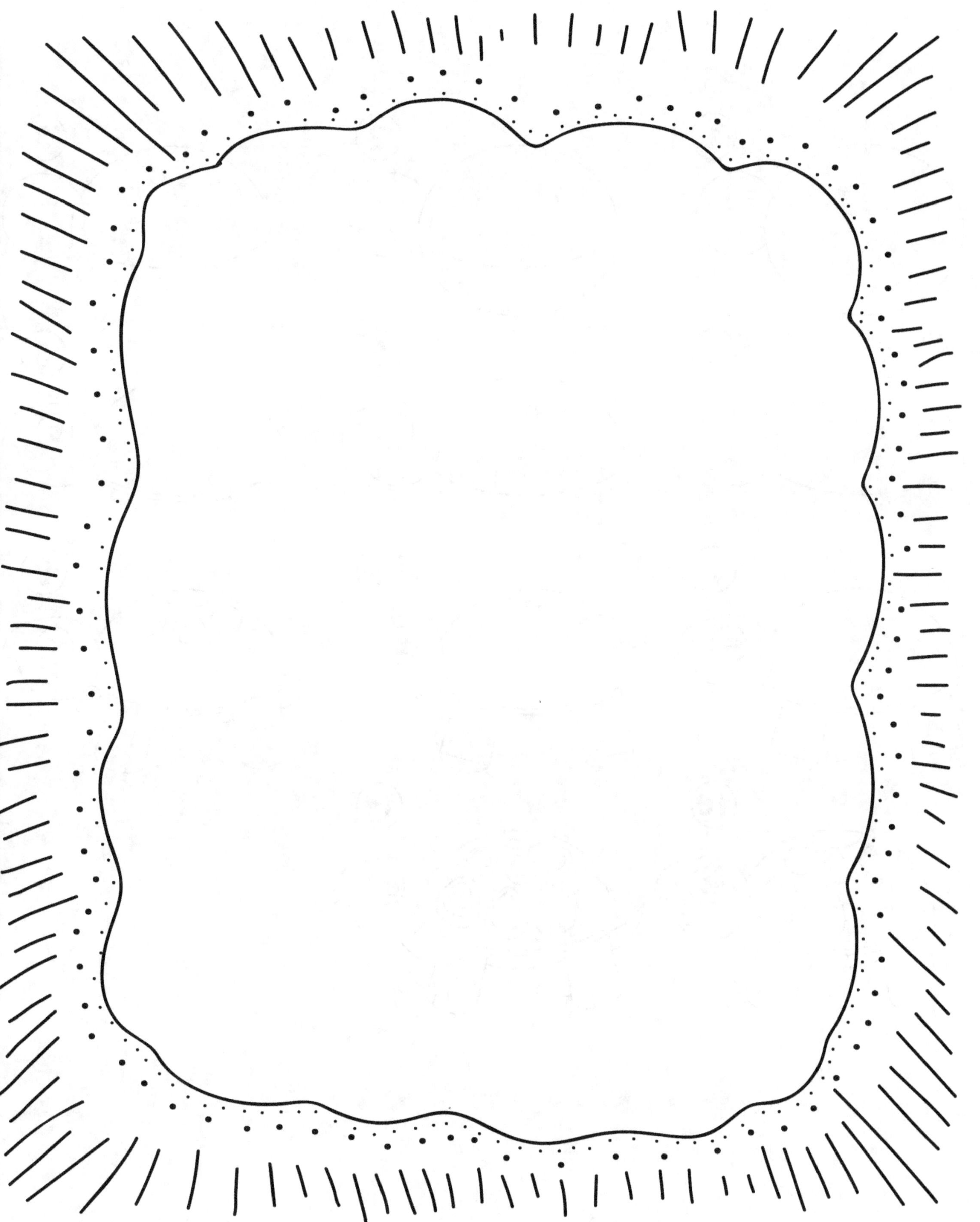

How to Draw a Turtle

Now You Try!

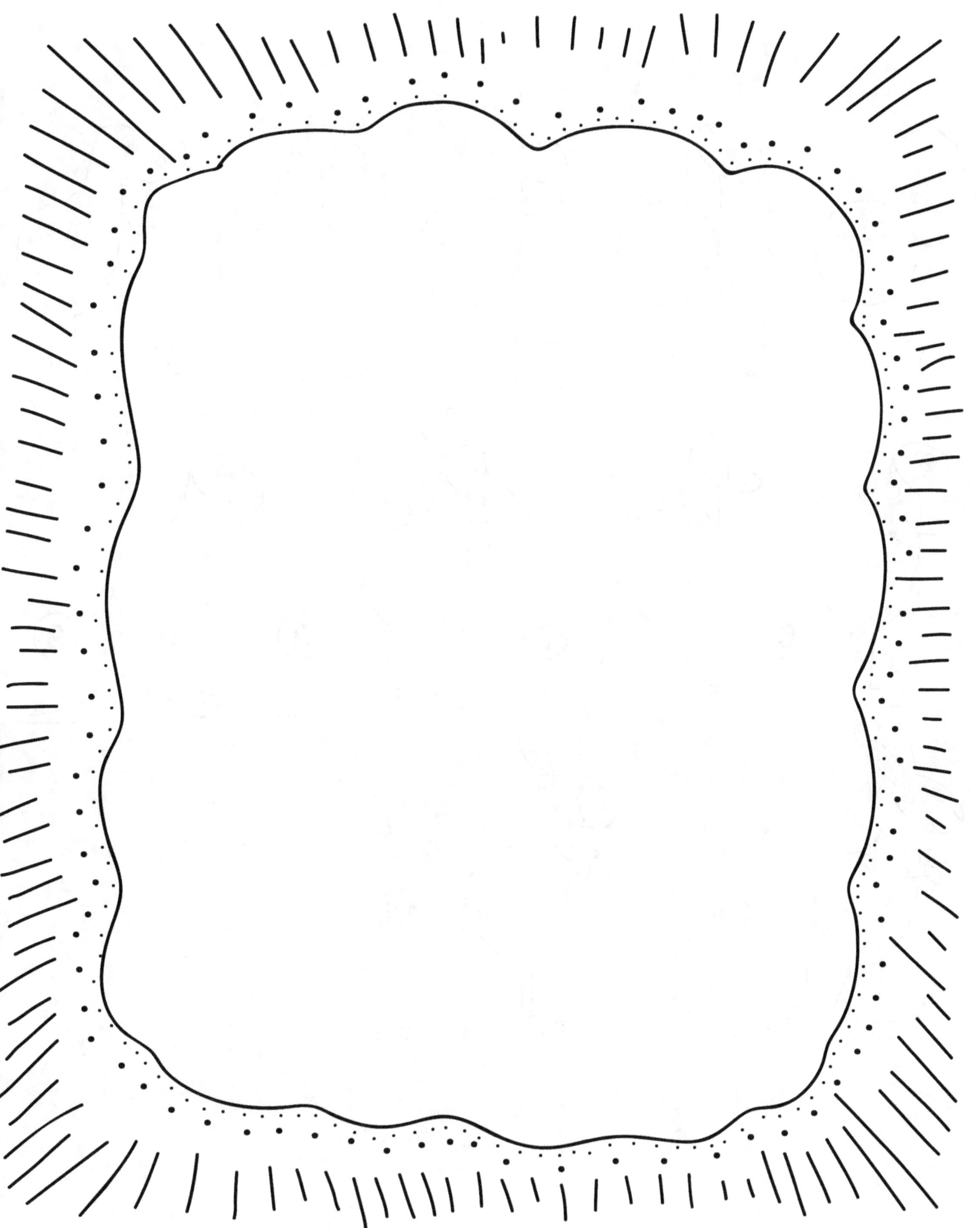

How to Draw a Kangaroo

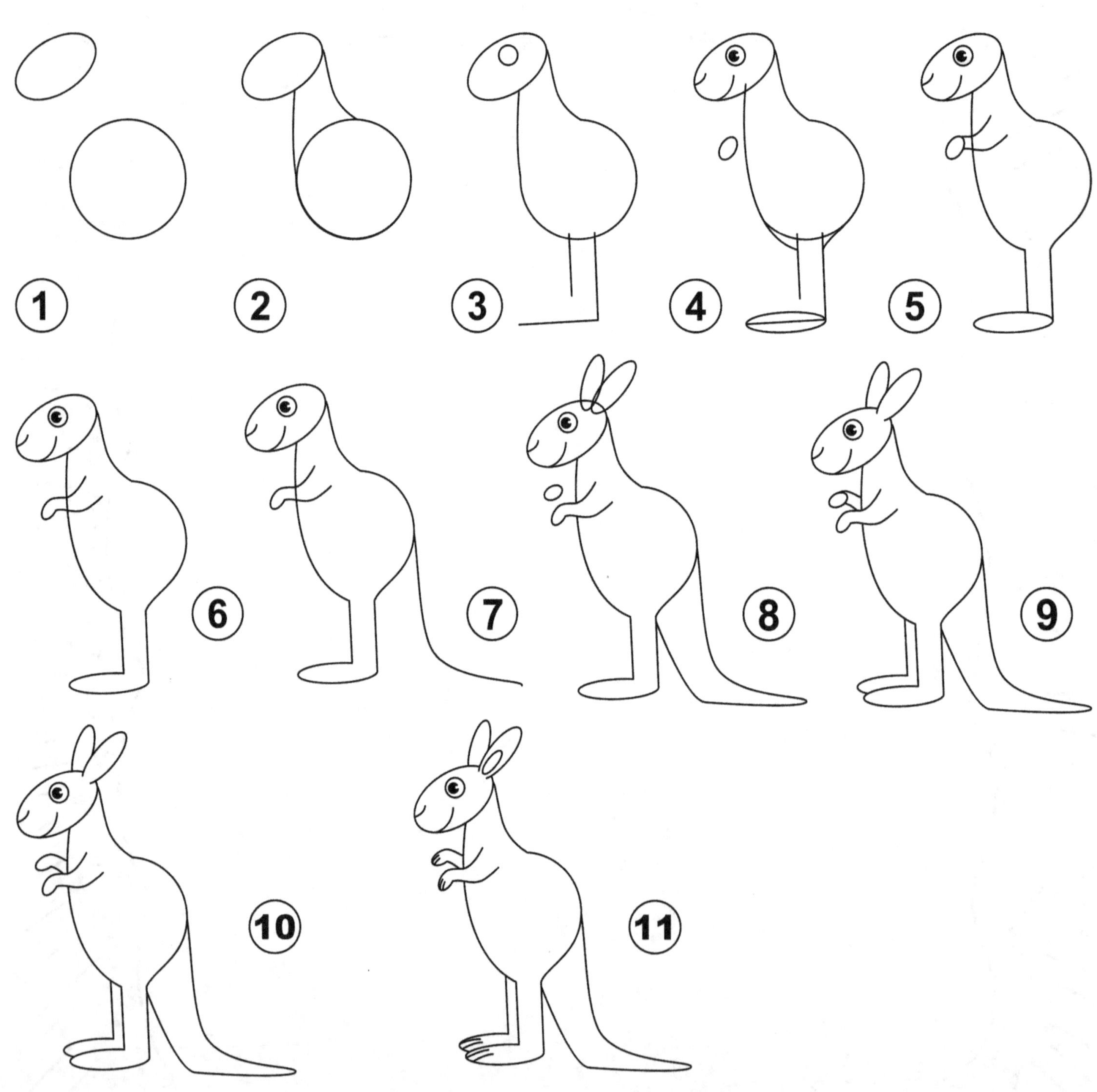

Now You Try!

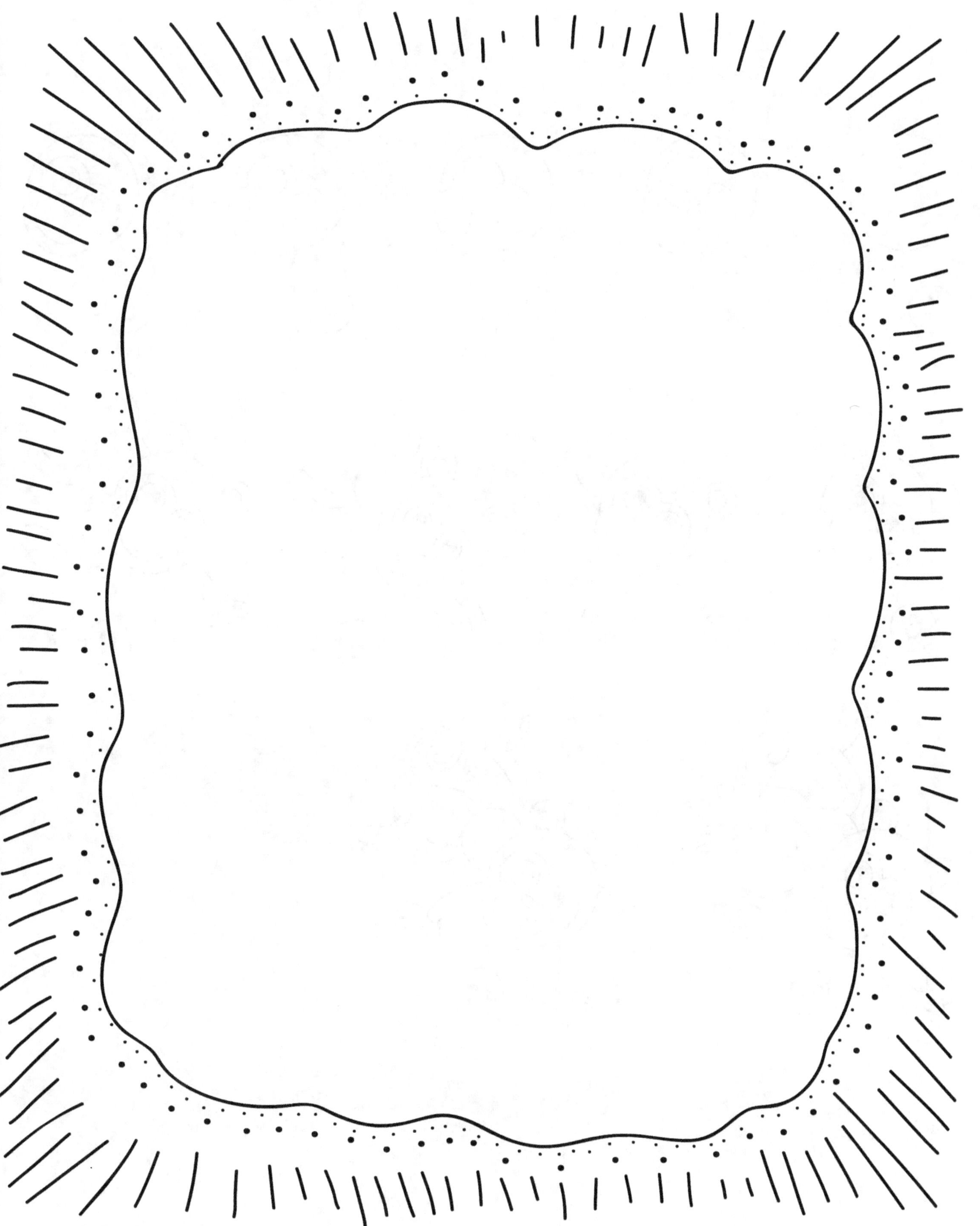

How to Draw a Monkey

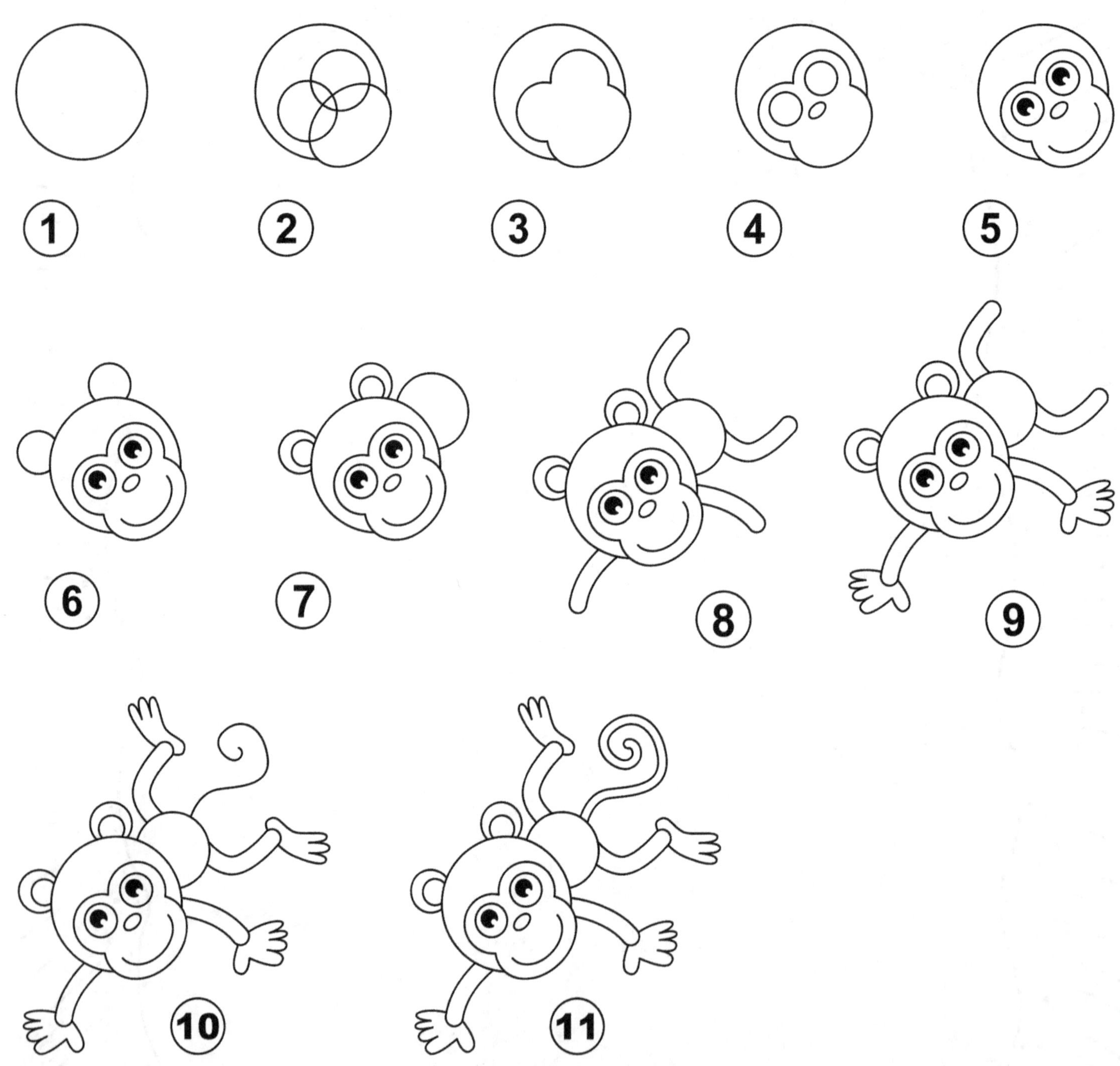

Now You Try!

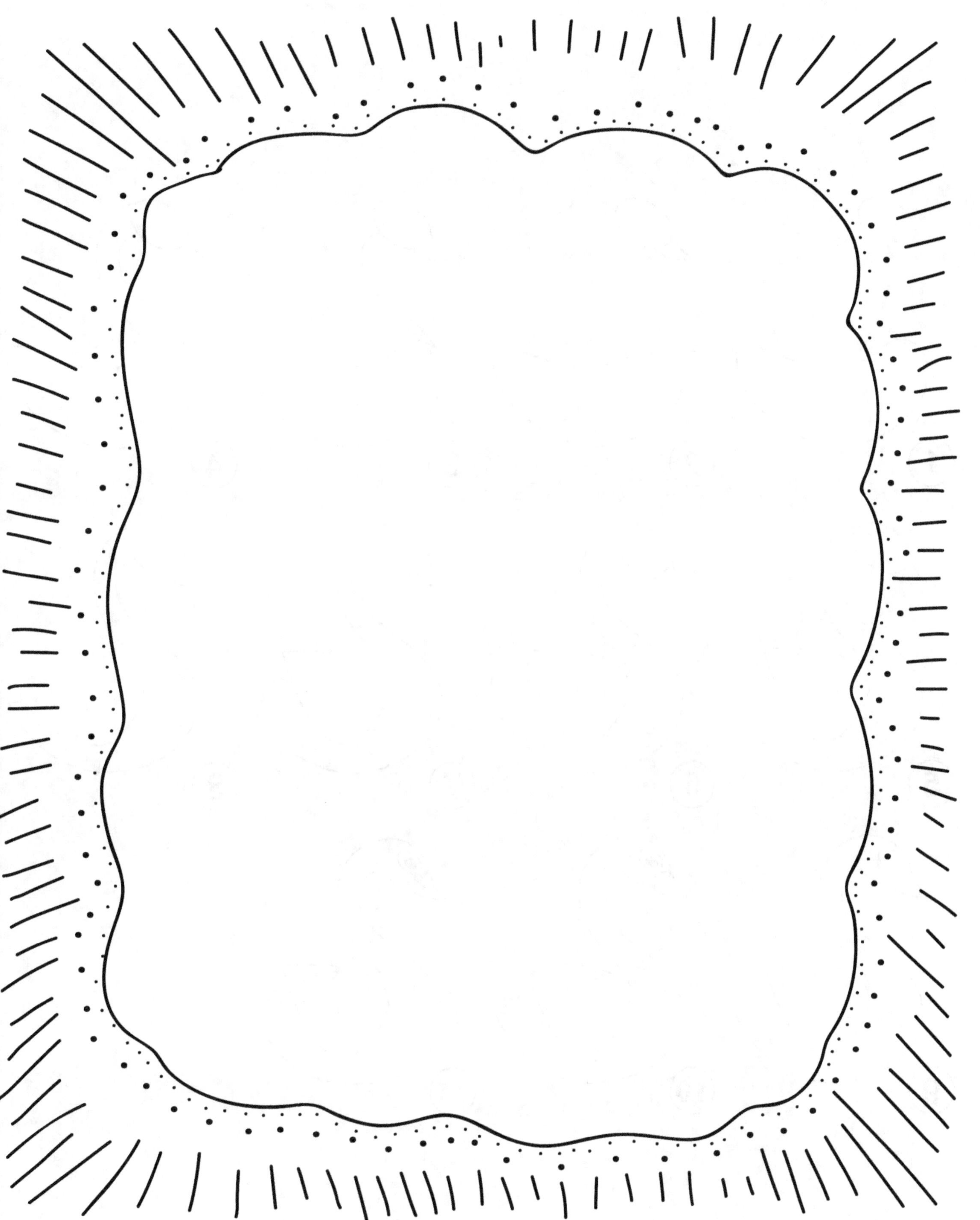

How to Draw a Swan

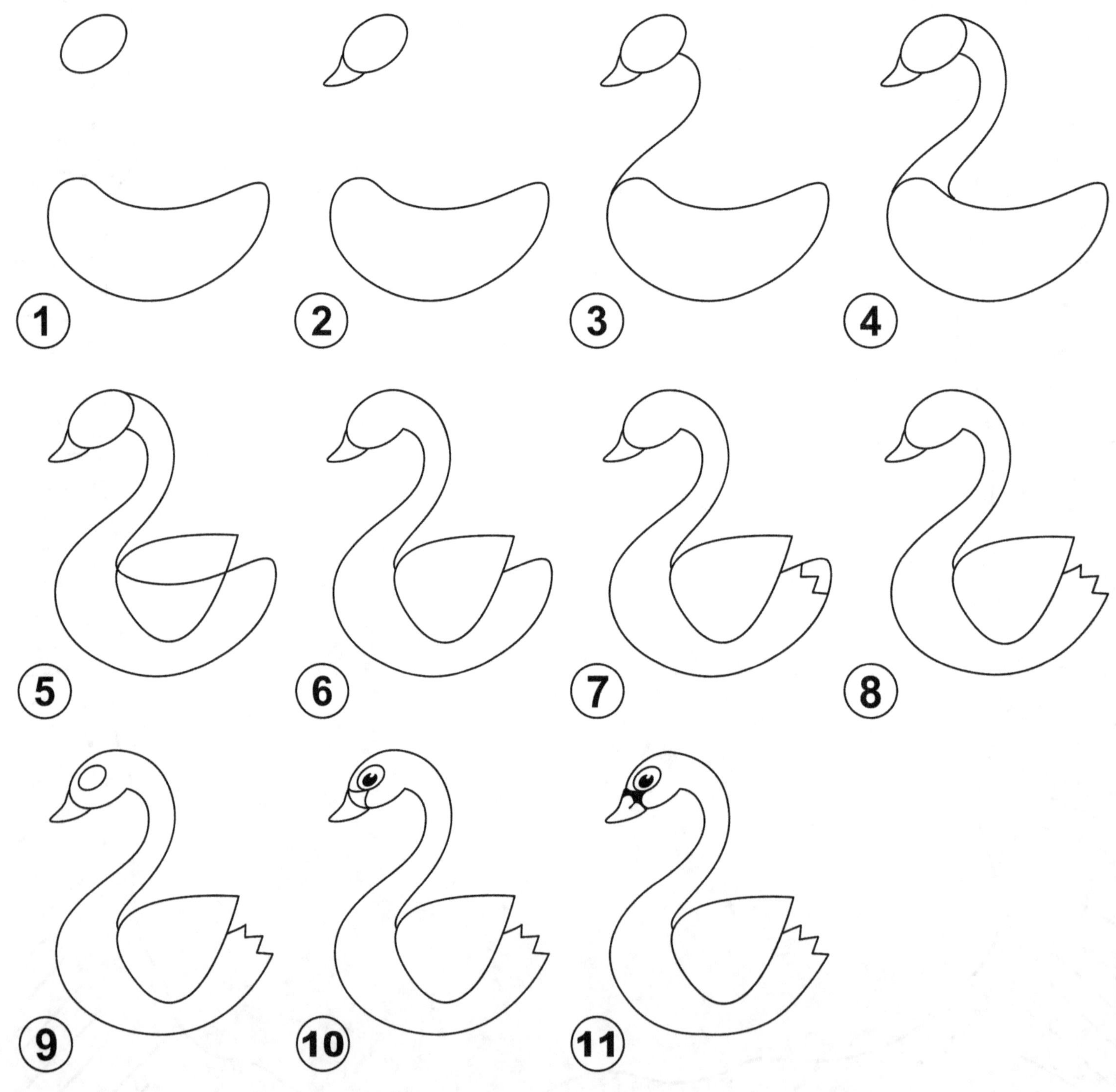

Now You Try!

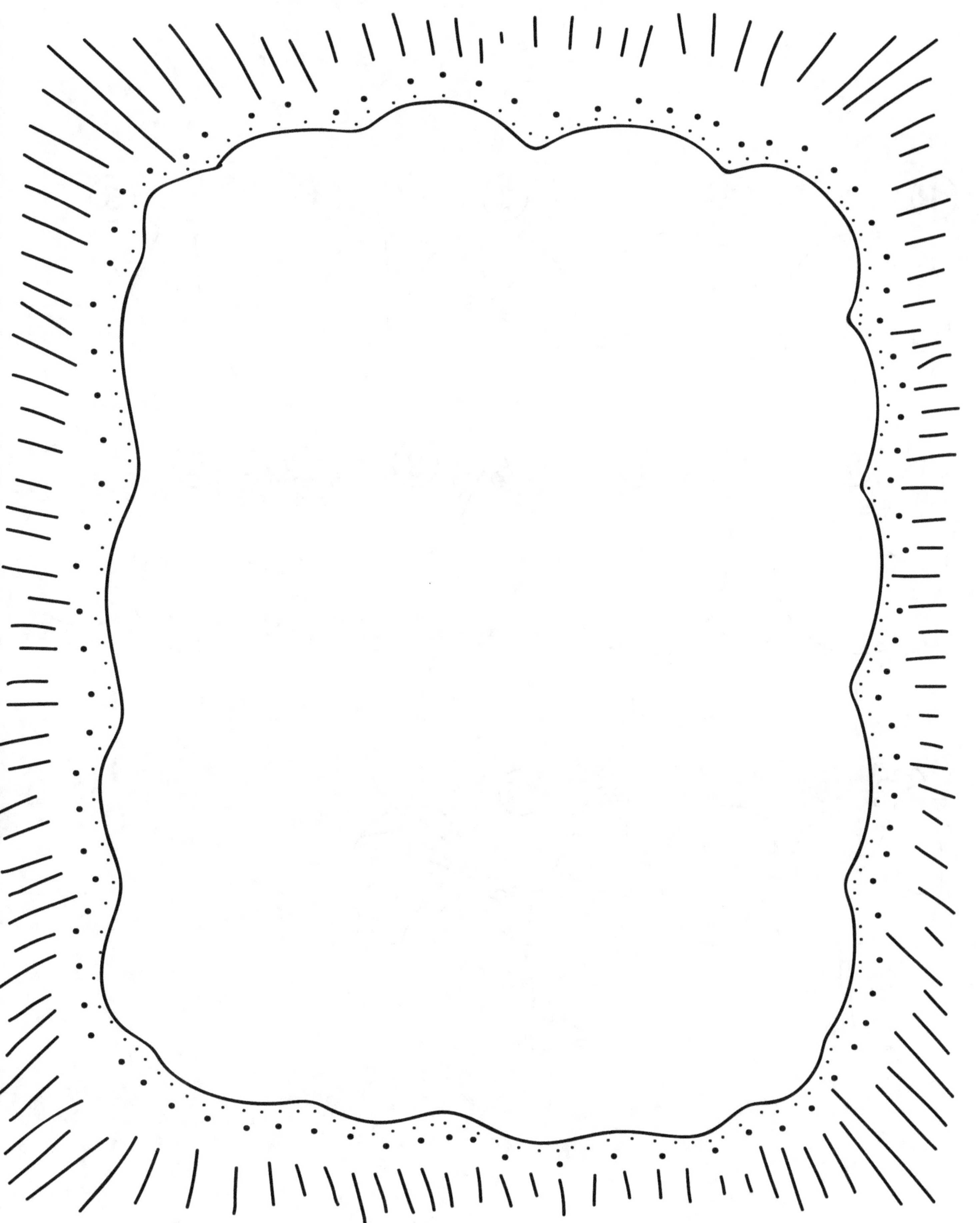

How to Draw a Rooster

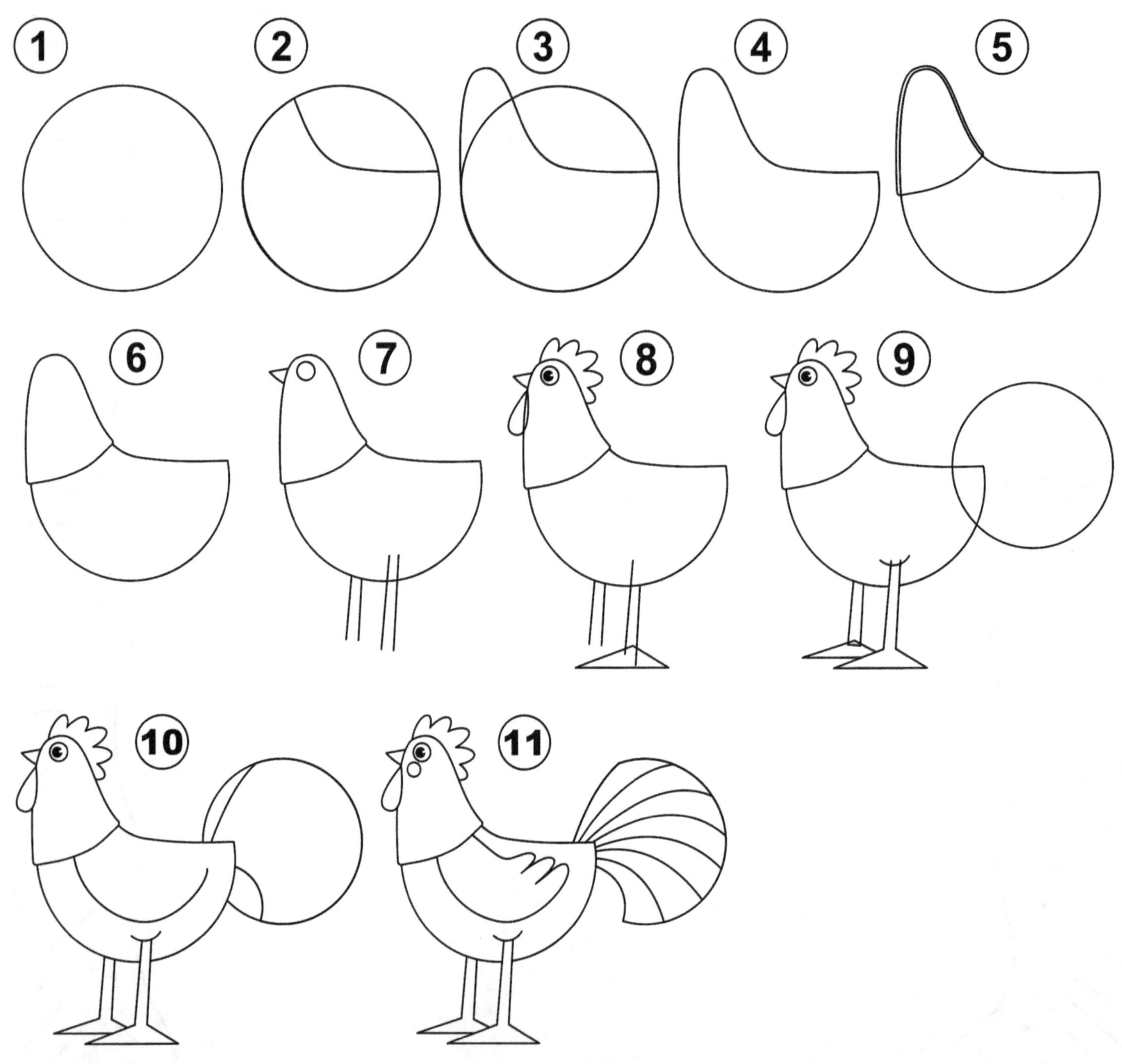

Now You Try!

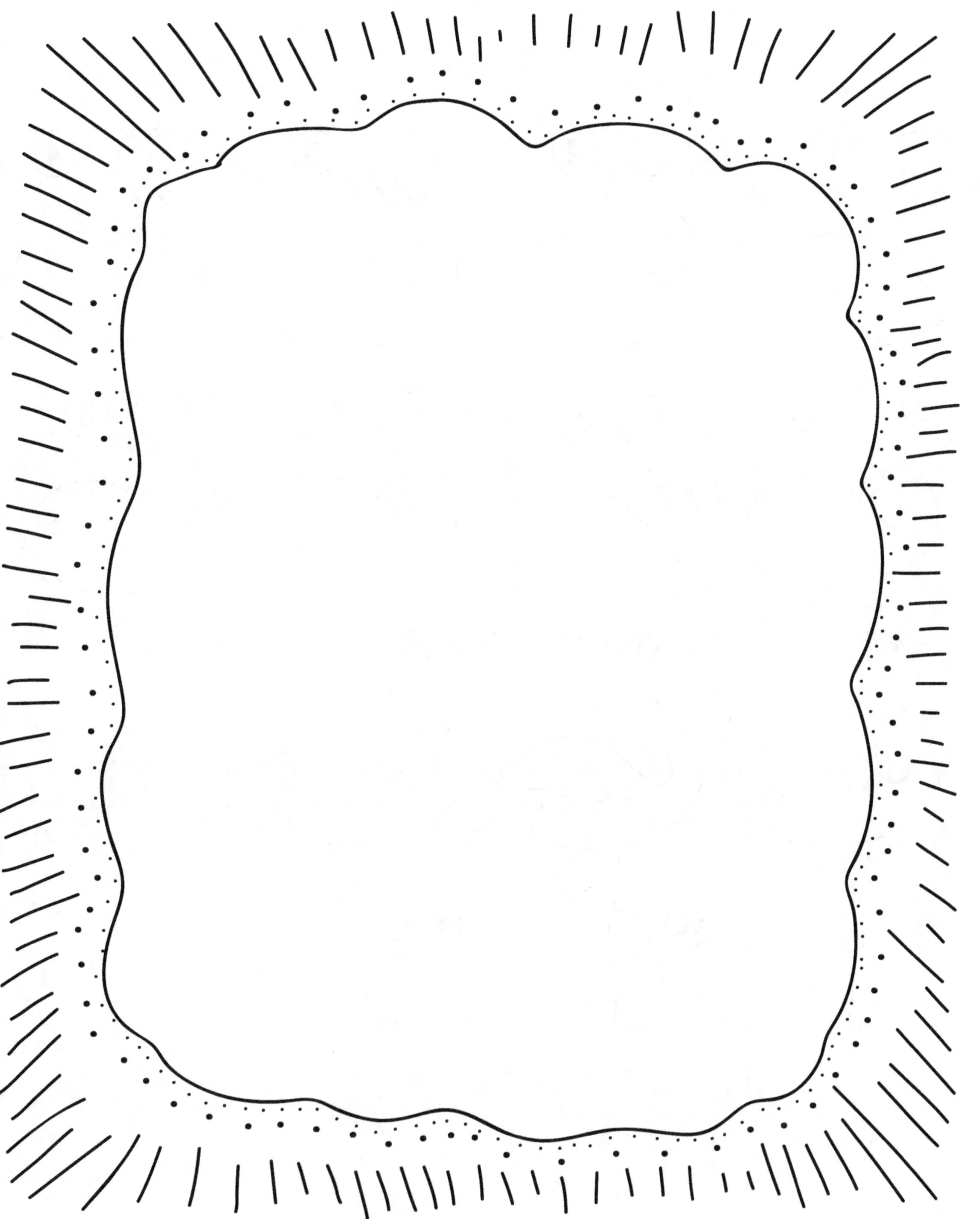

How to Draw a Flamingo

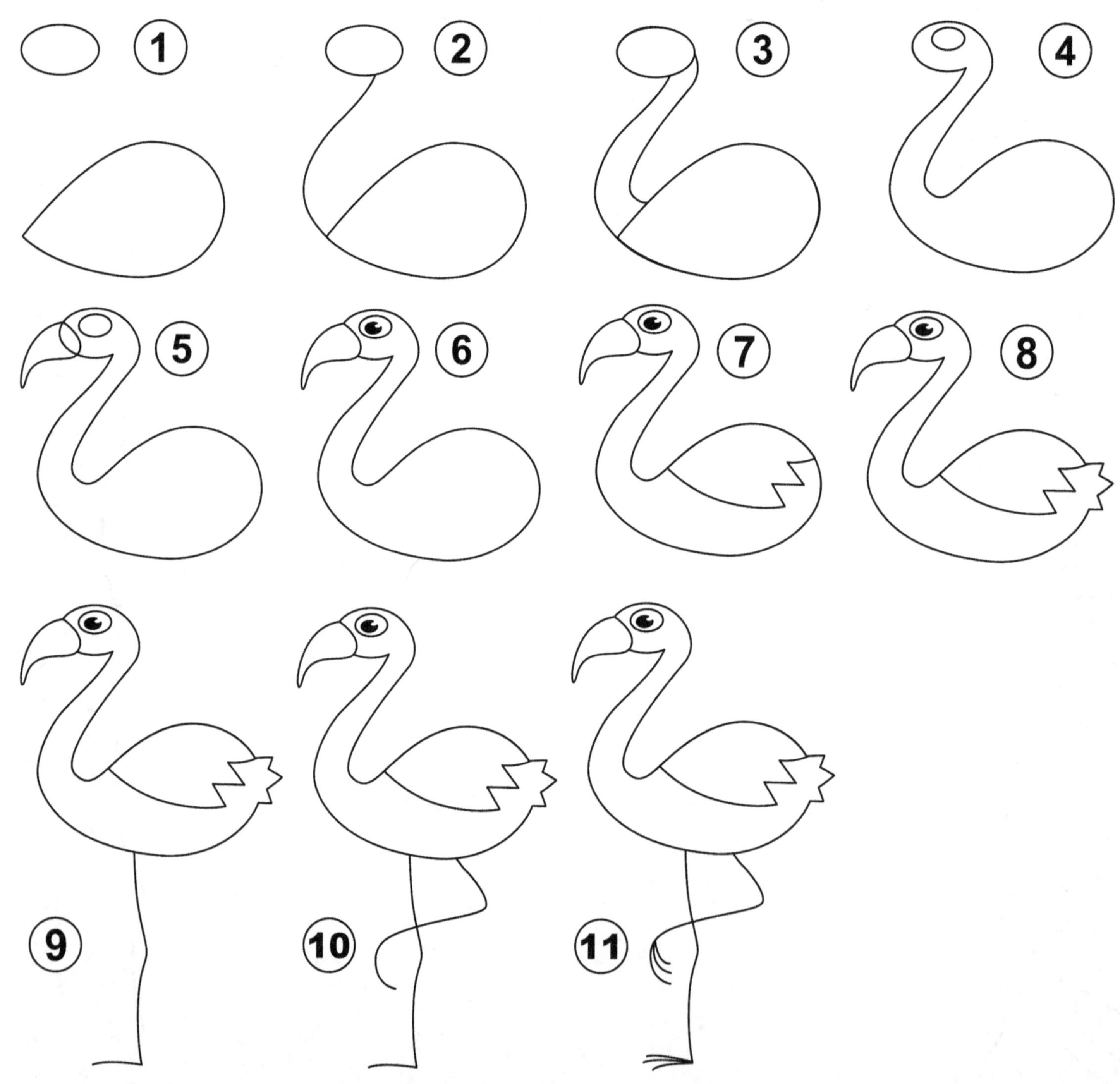

Now You Try!

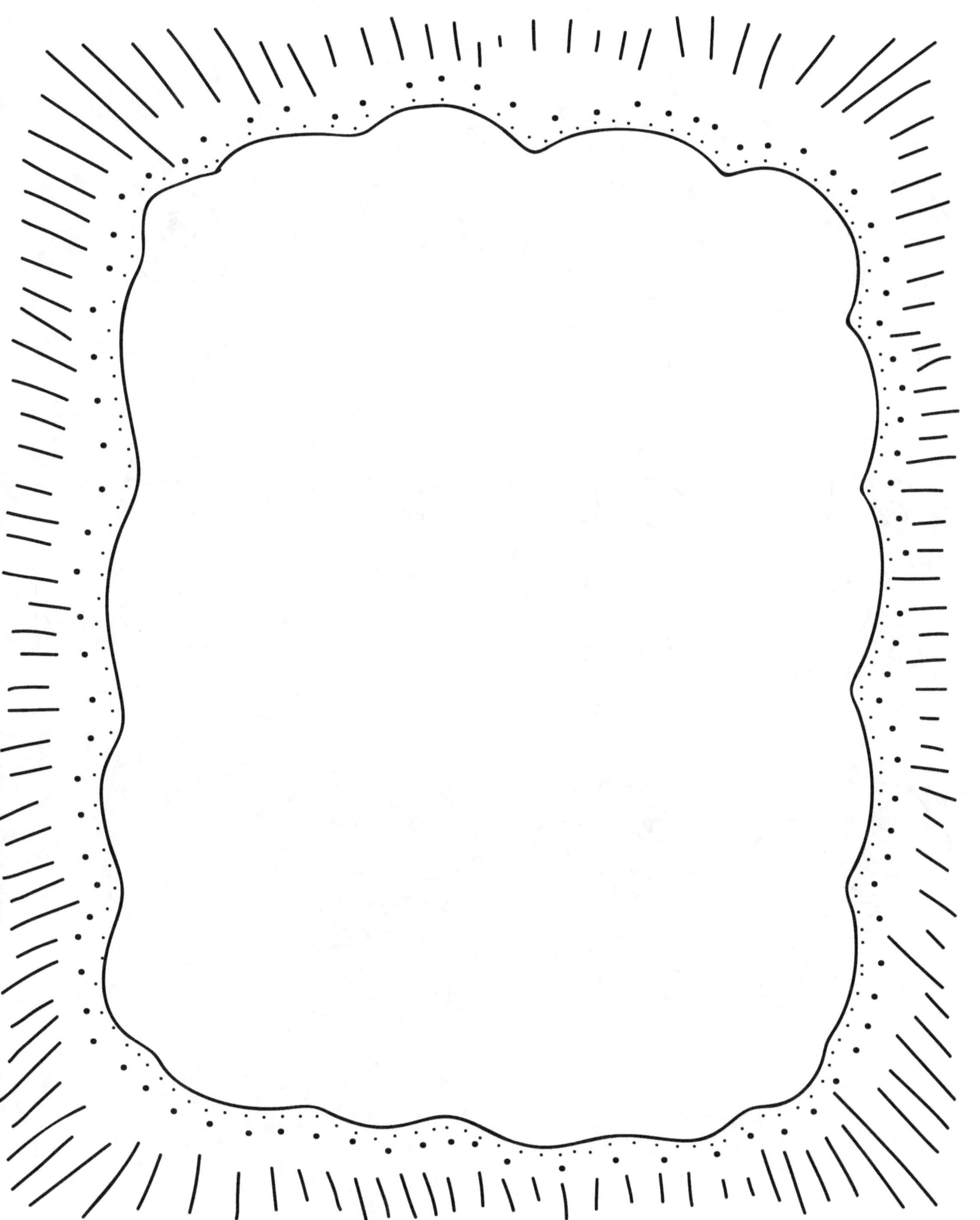

How to Draw an Iguana

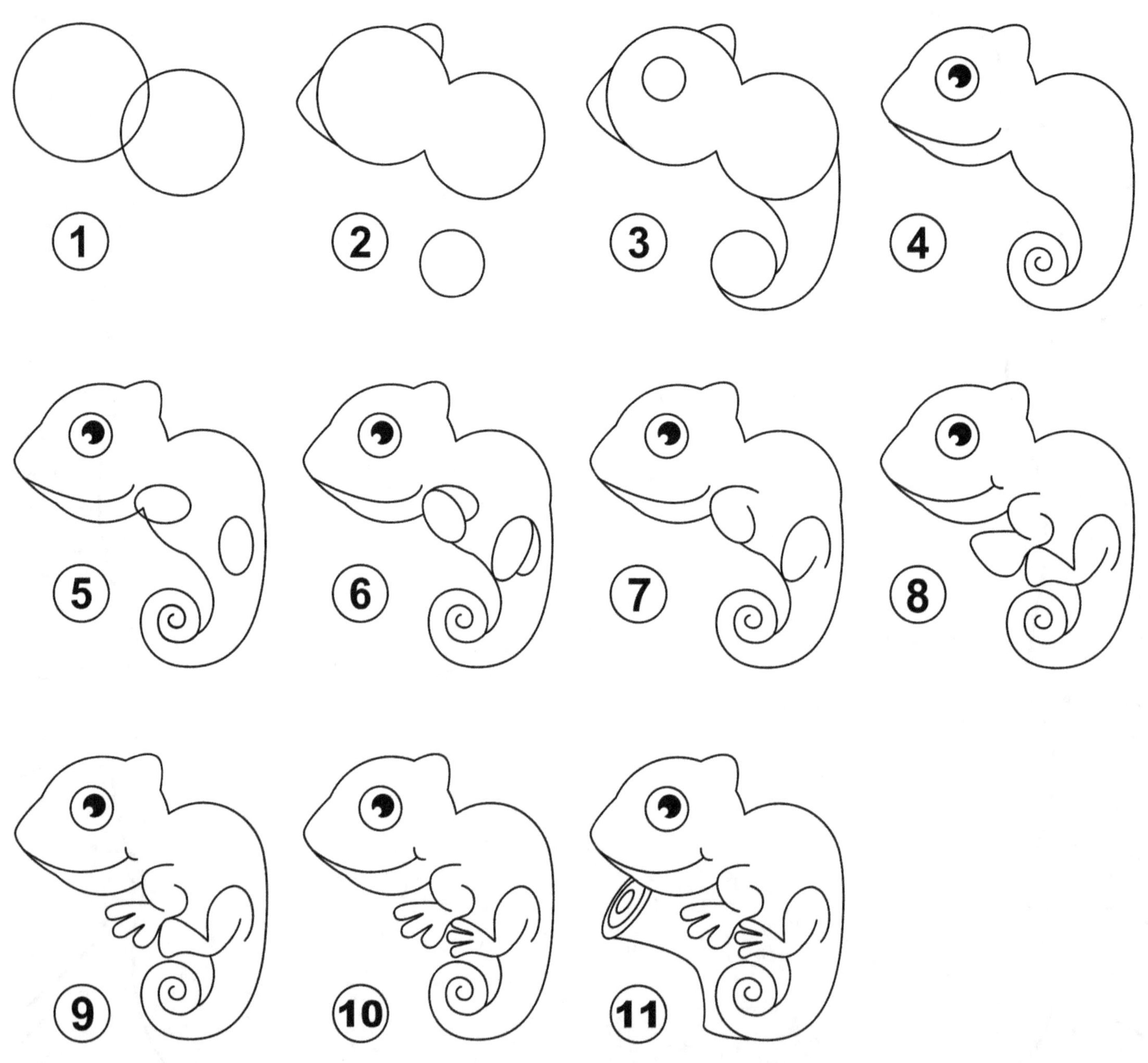

Now You Try!

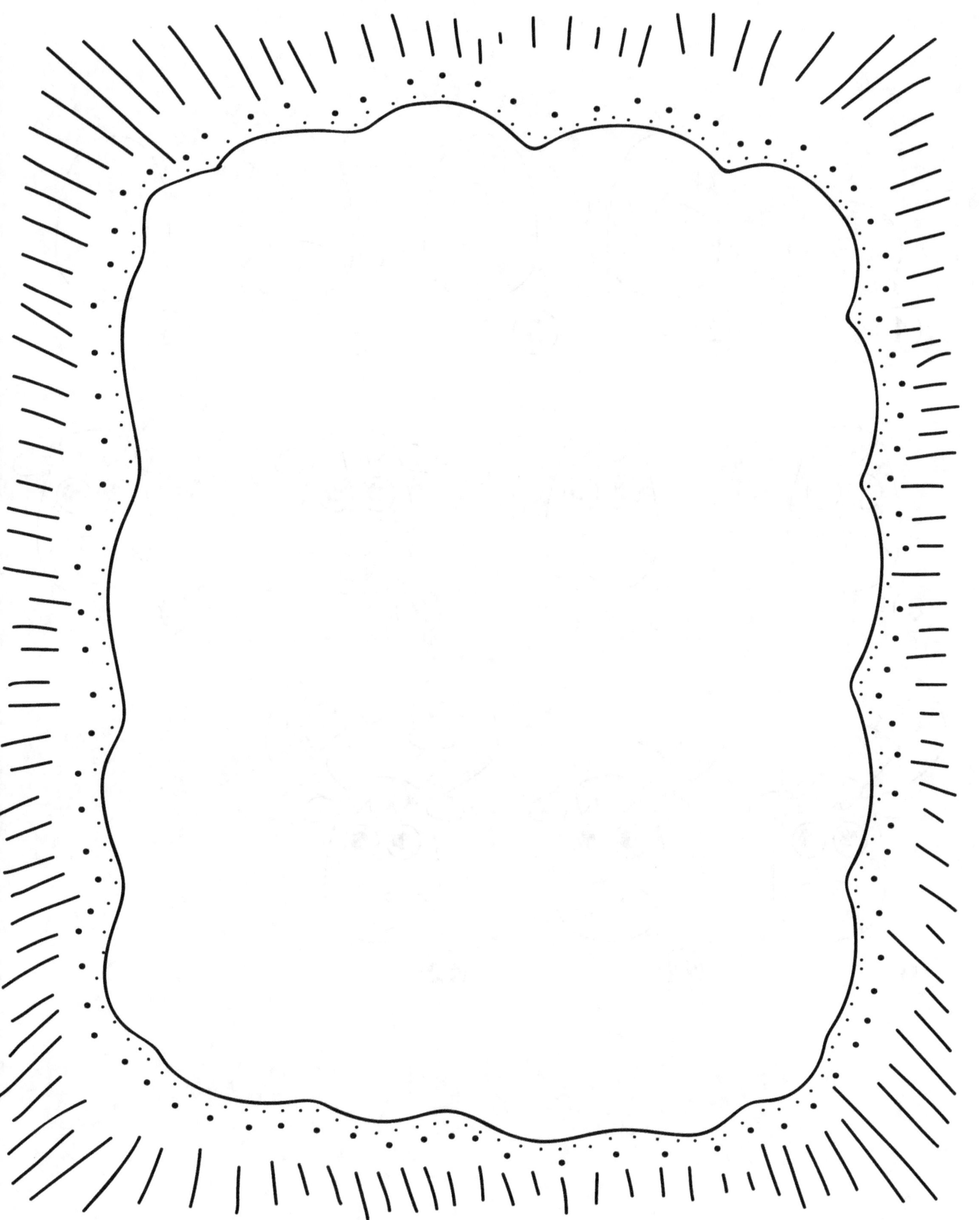

How to Draw an Elk

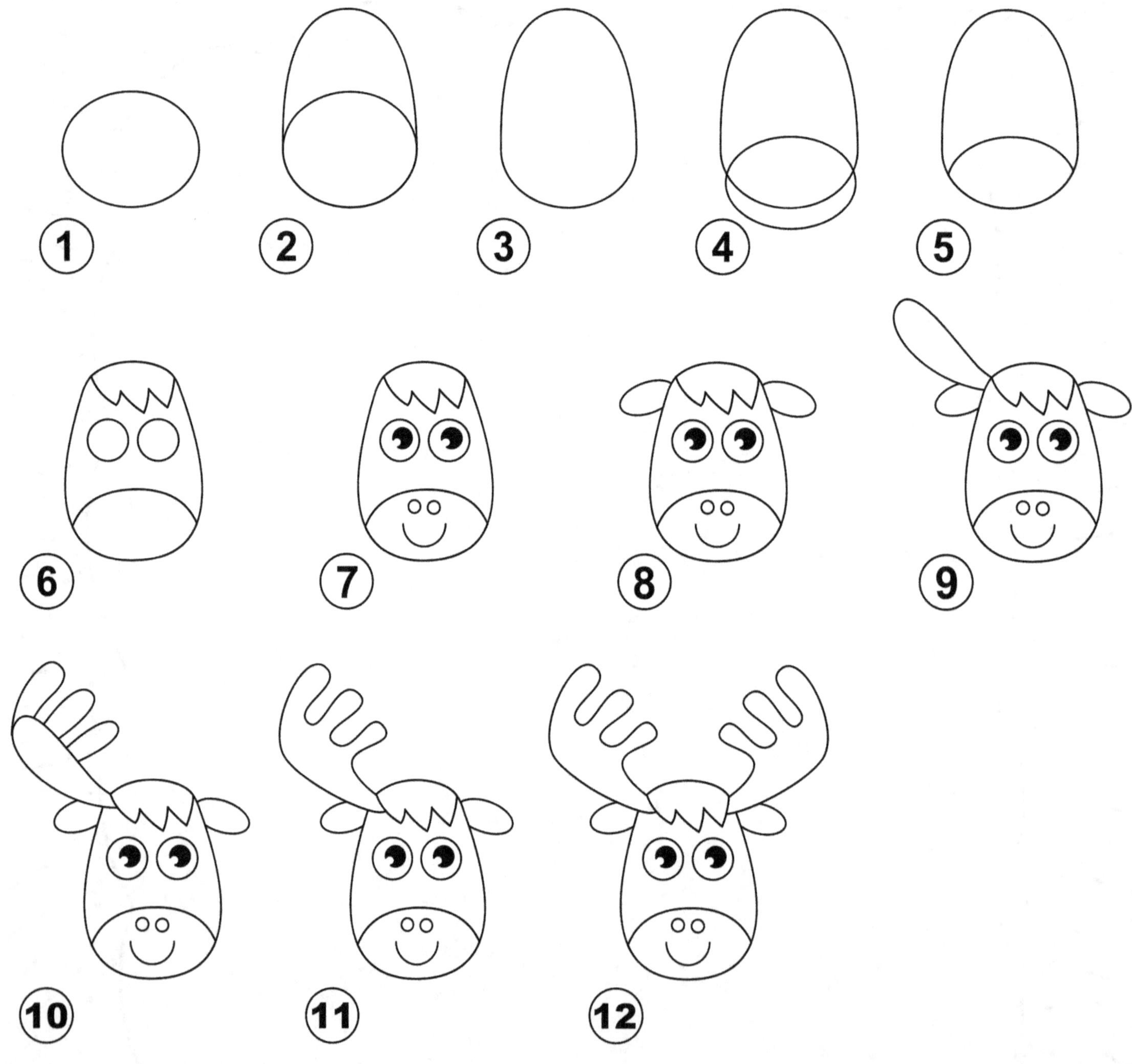

Now You Try!

How to Draw a Koala

Now You Try!

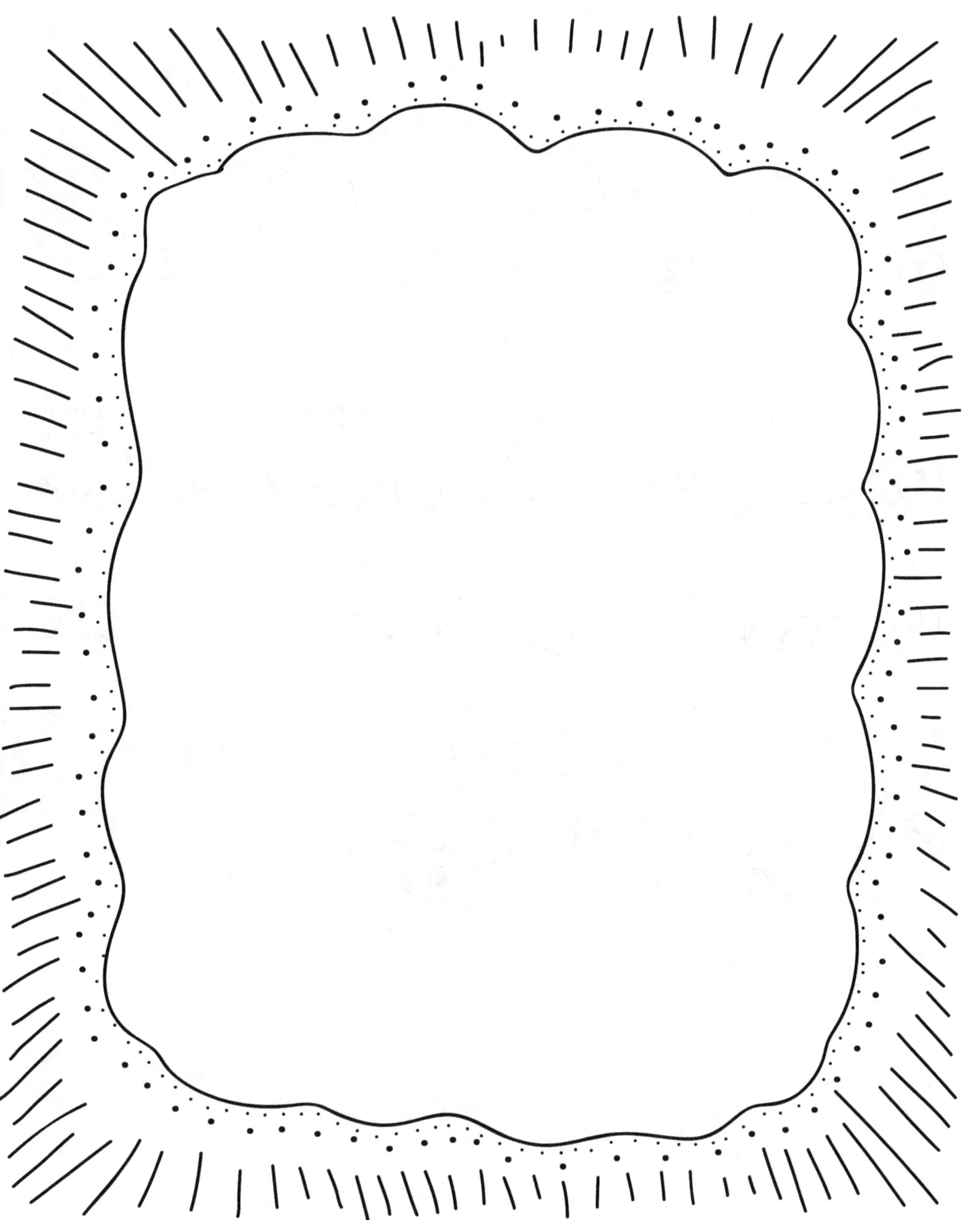

How to Draw an Ox

Now You Try!

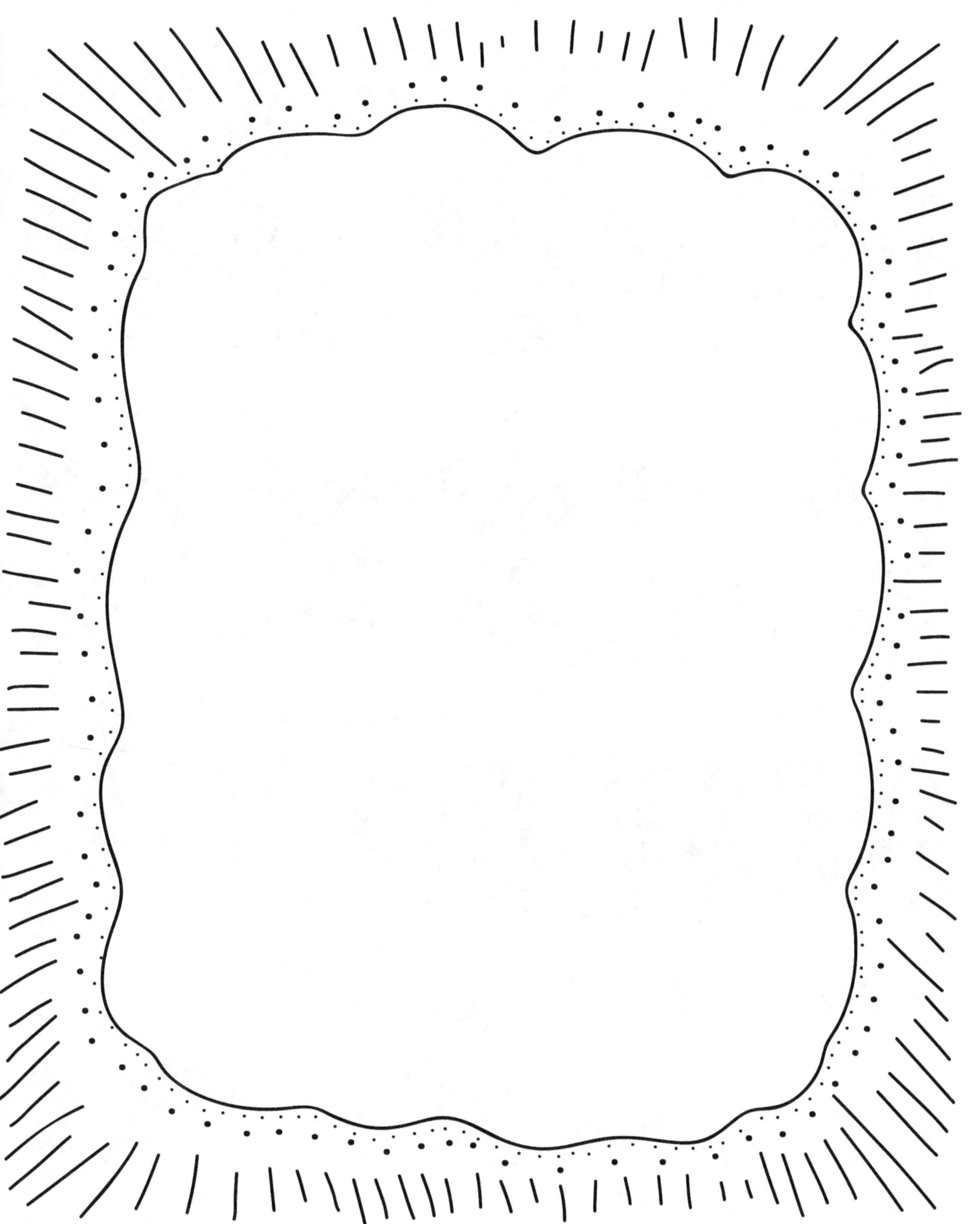

How to Draw a Unicorn

Now You Try!

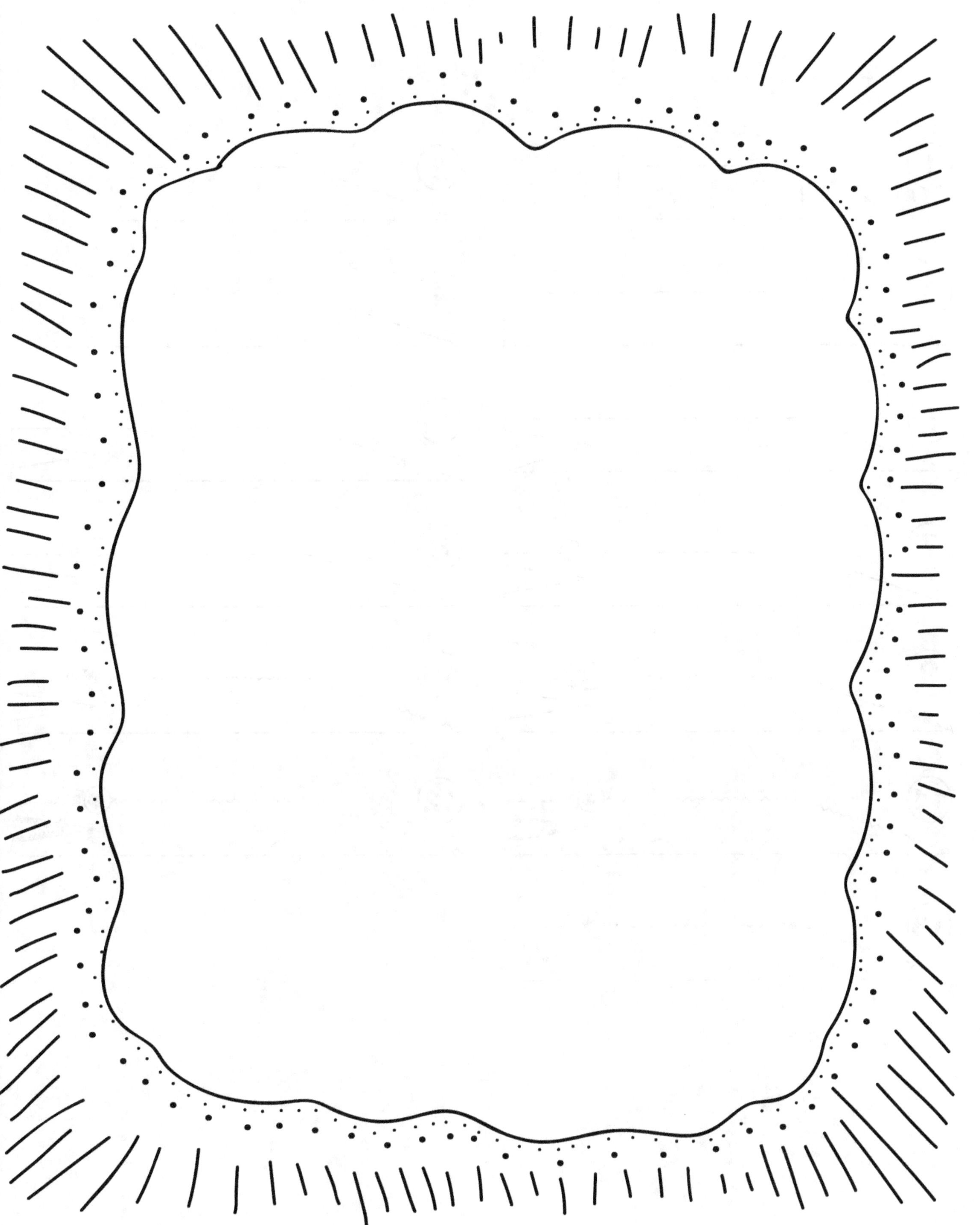

How to Draw an Alligator

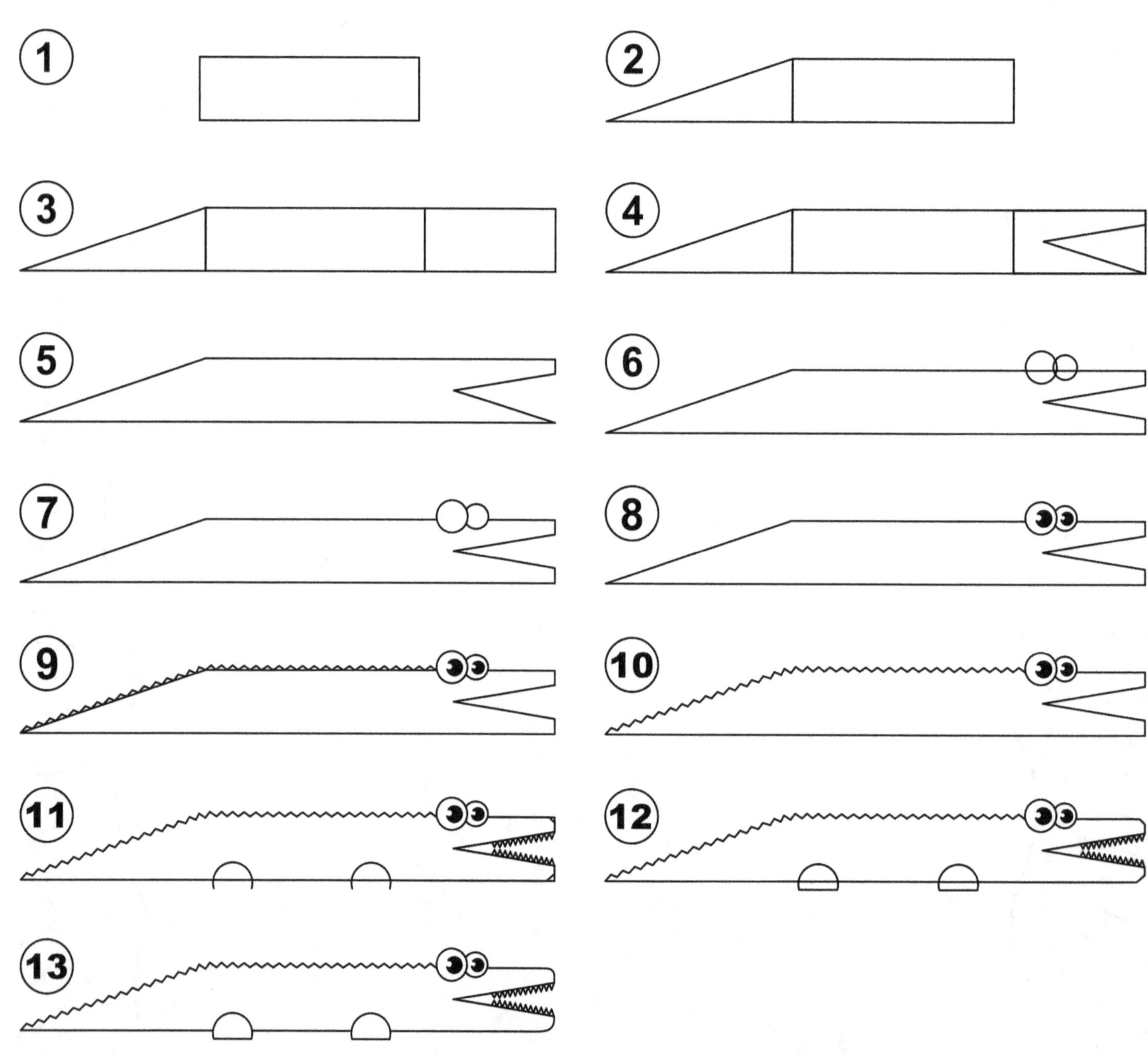

Now You Try!

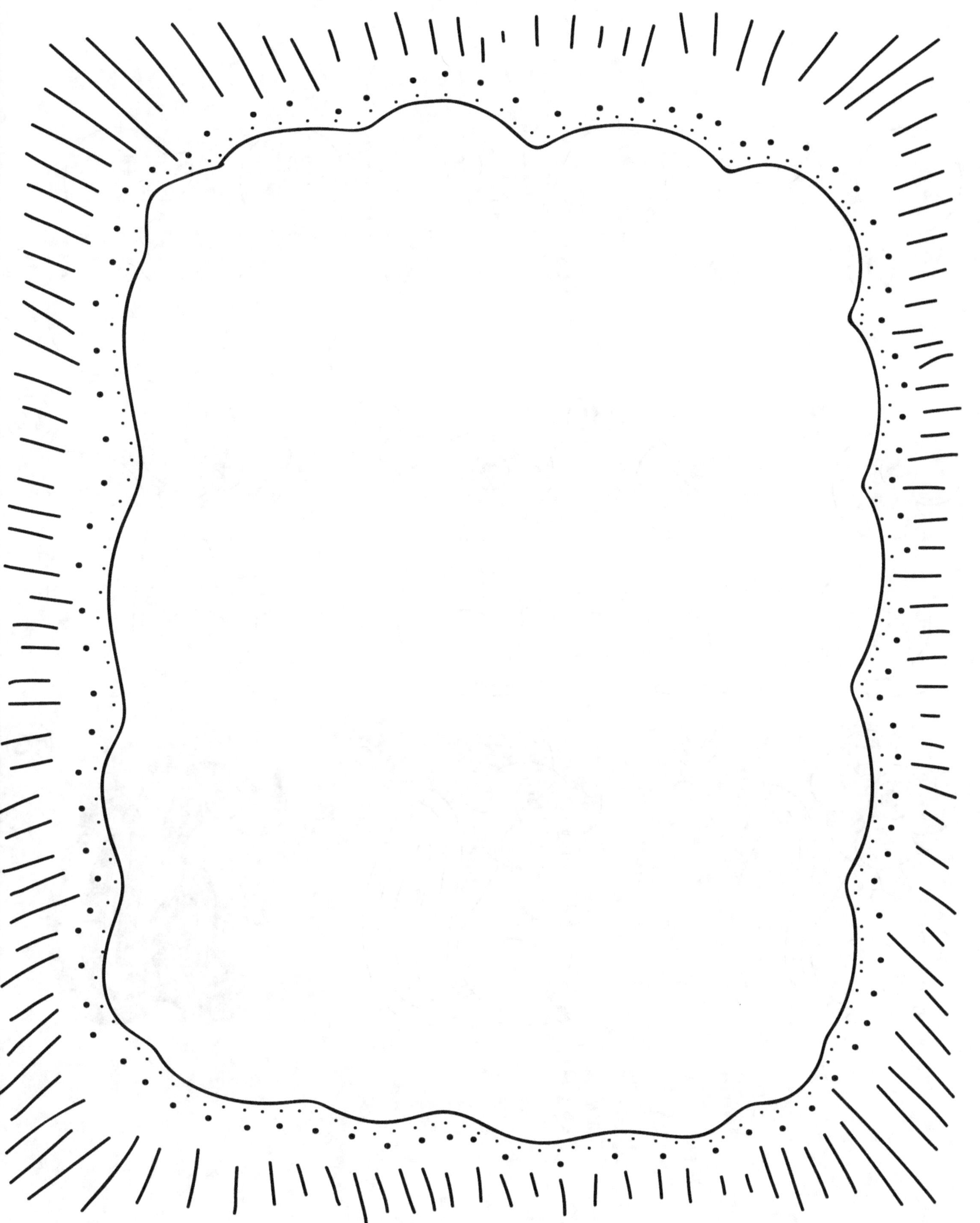

How to Draw a Skunk

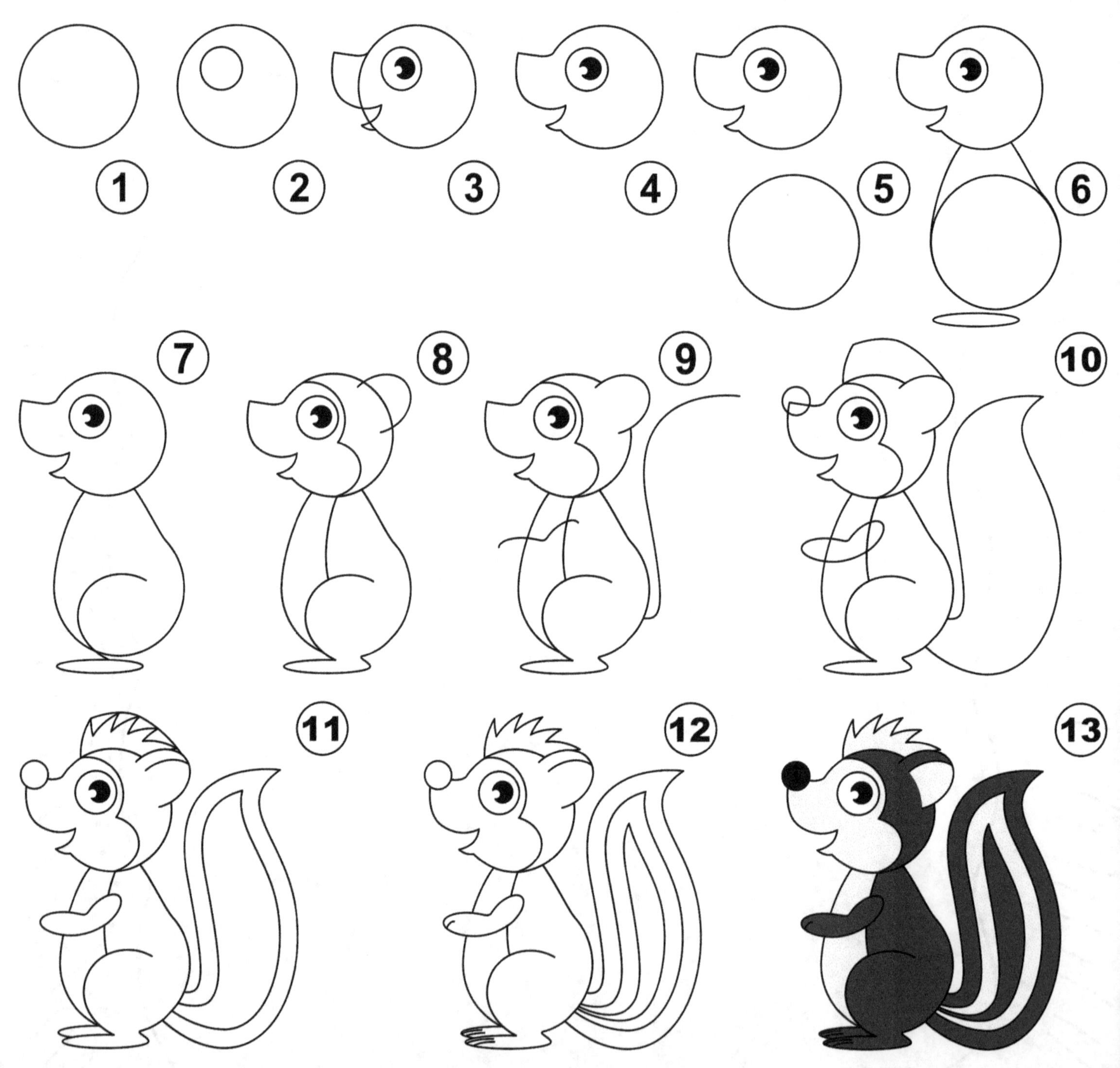

Now You Try!

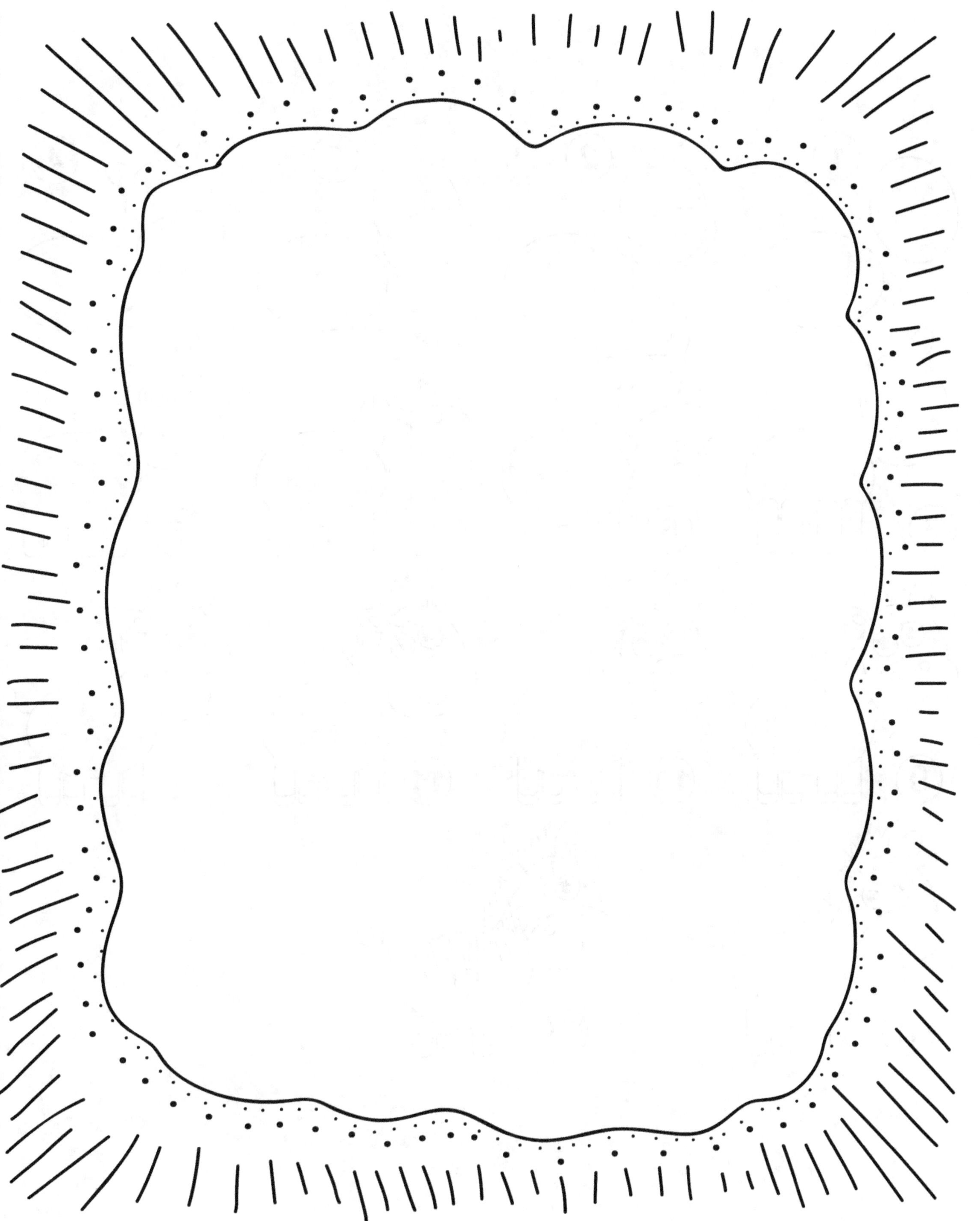

How to Draw a Zebra

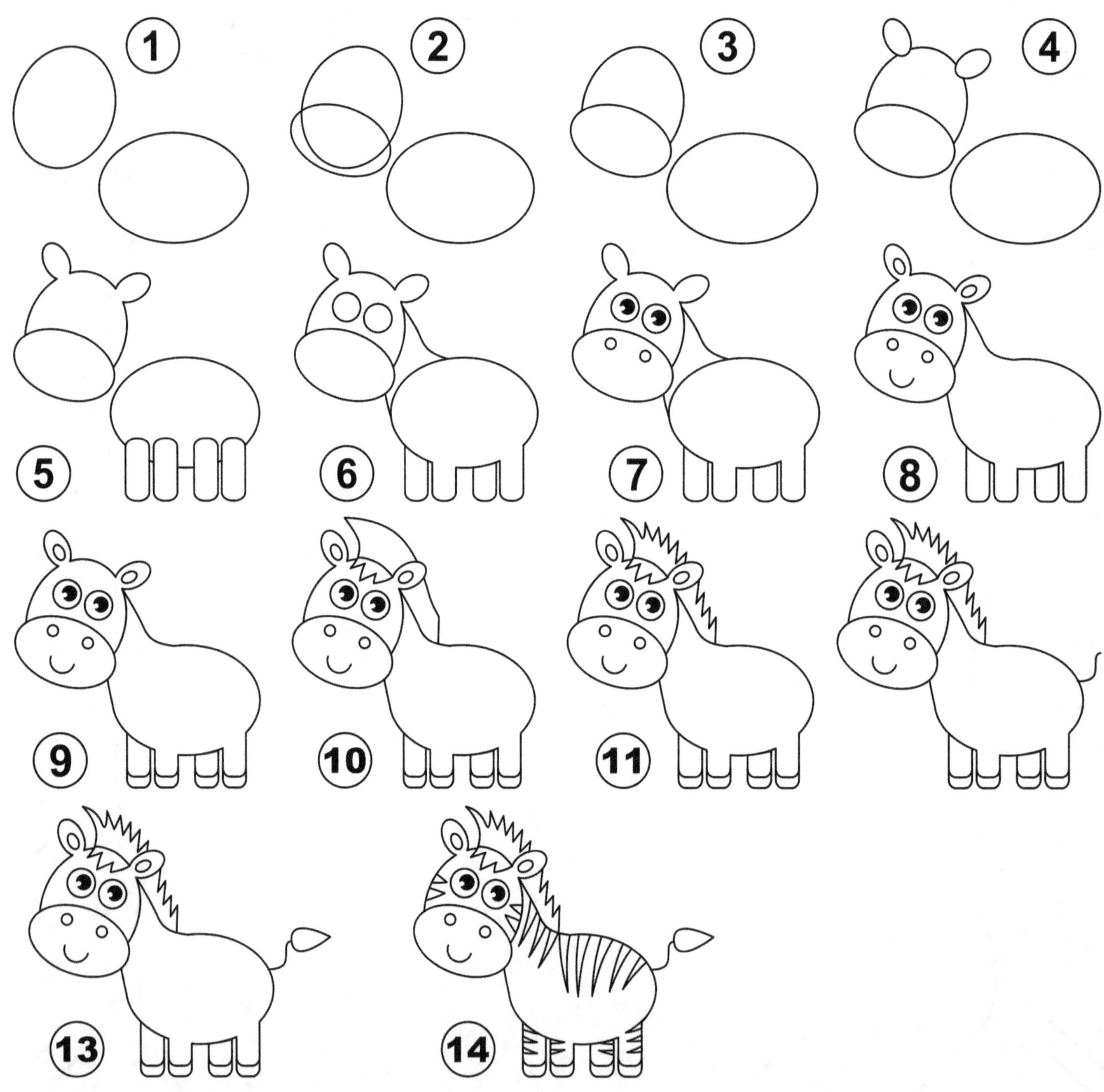

Now You Try!

How to Draw a Bat

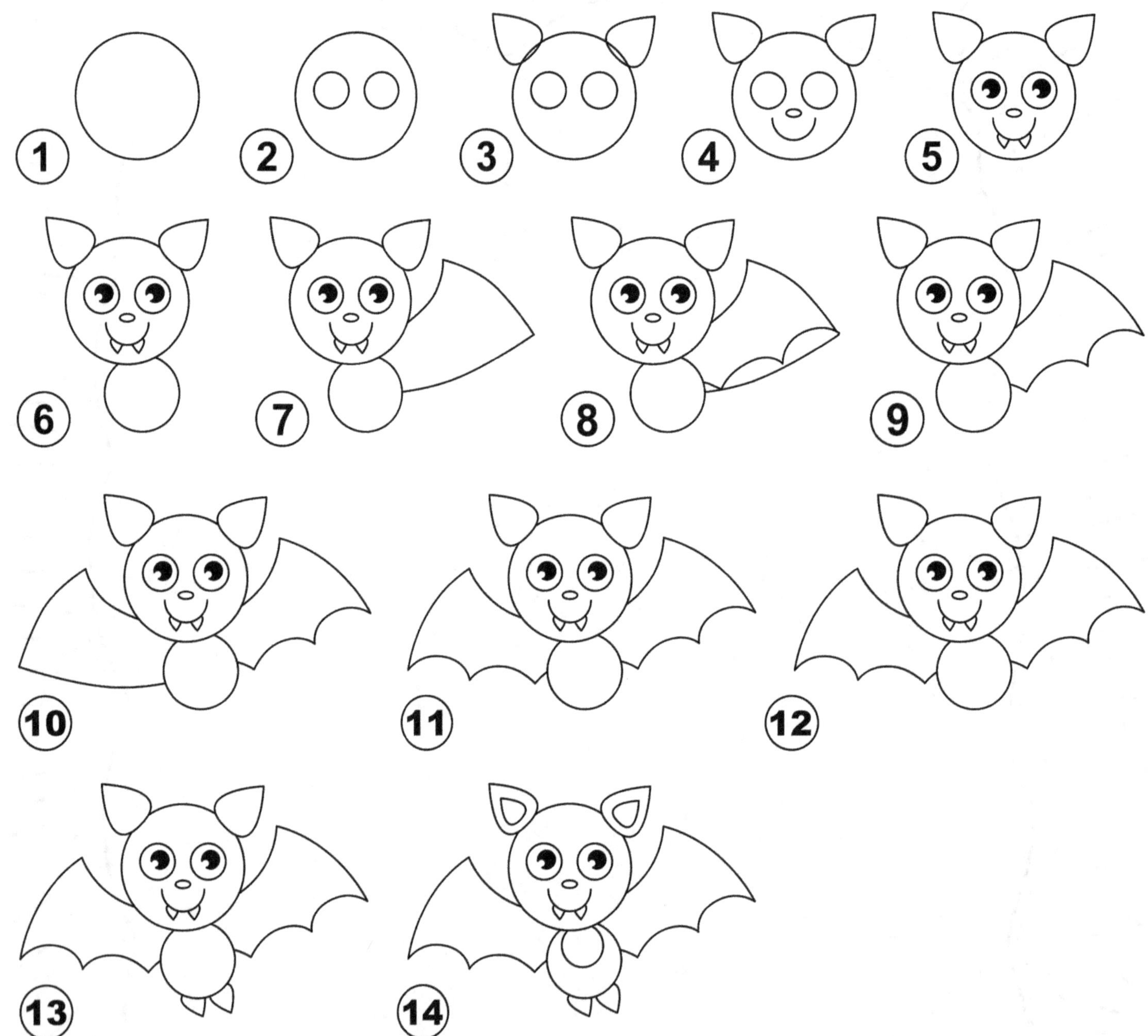

Now You Try!

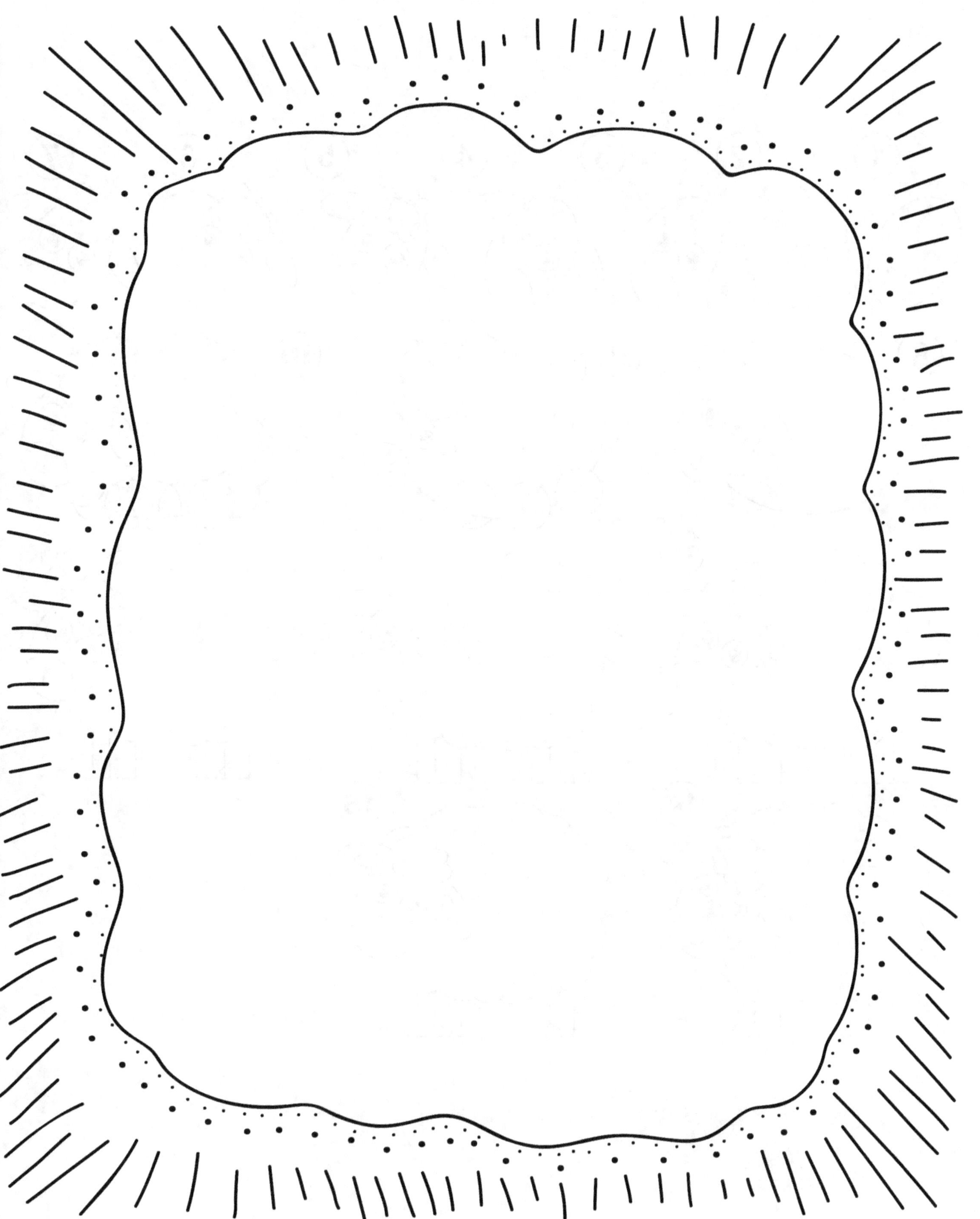

How to Draw a Sheep

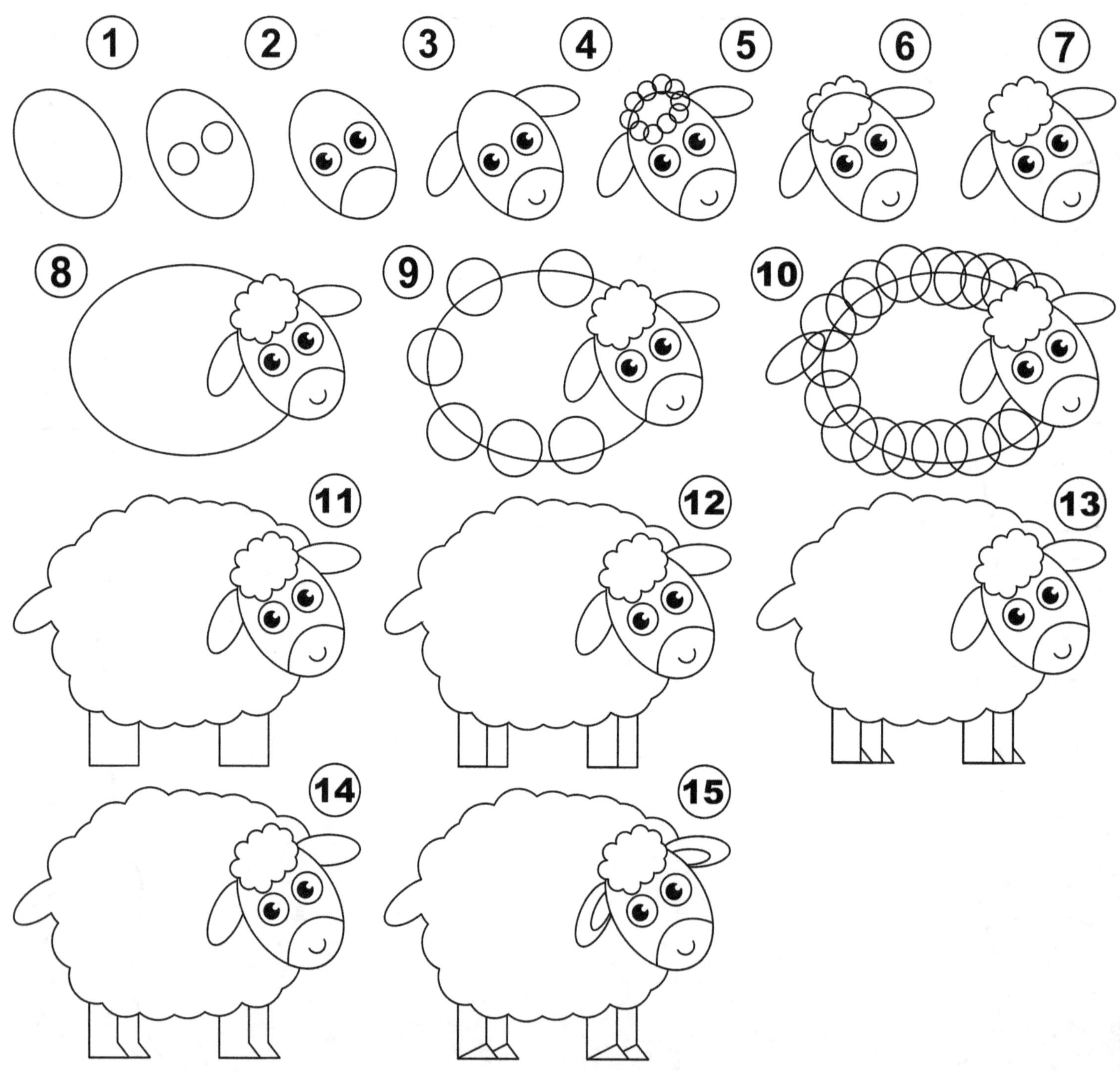

Now You Try!

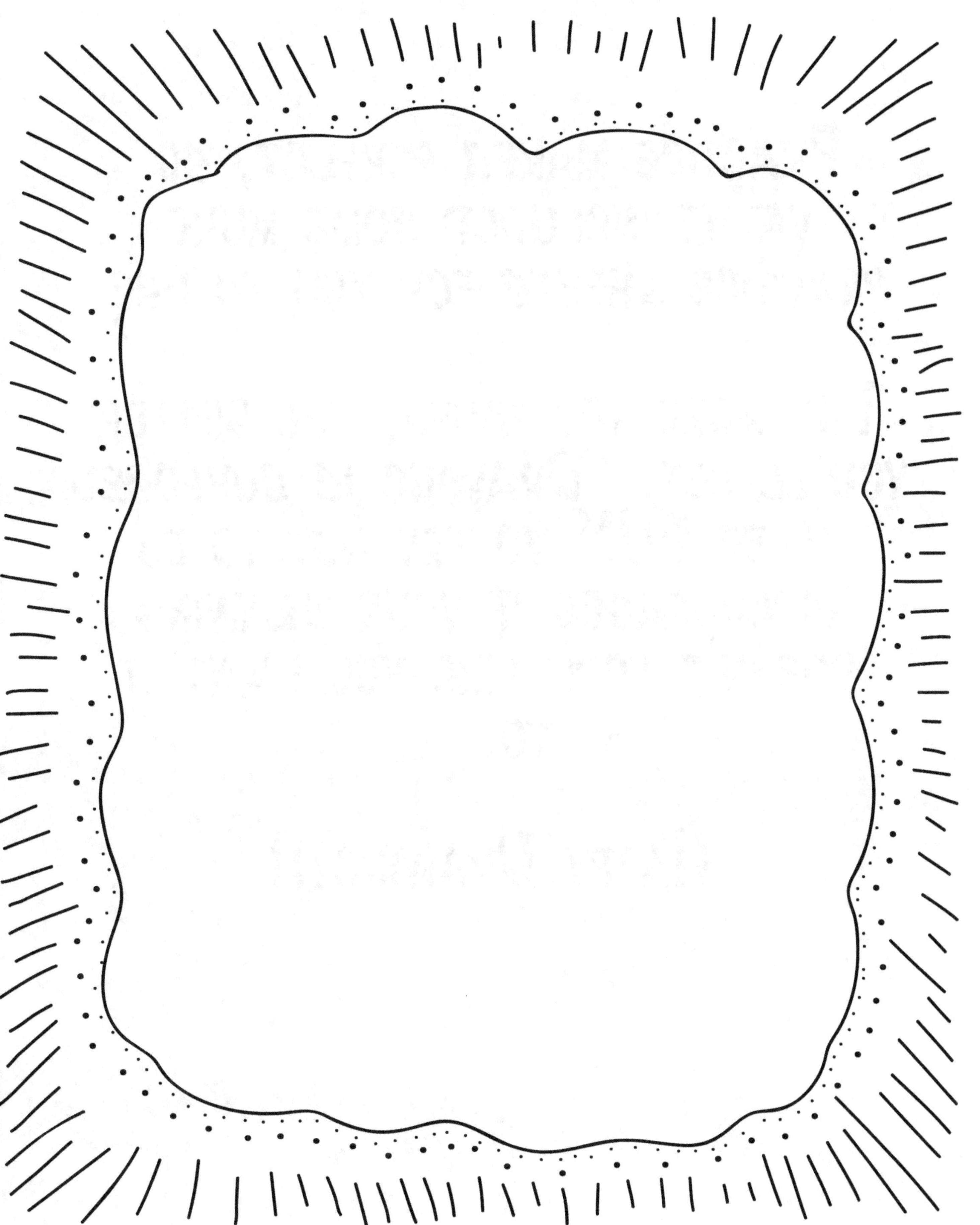

PRACTICE MAKES PERFECT, SO WE'VE INCLUDED SOME MORE PRACTICE SHEETS FOR YOU TO USE.

THE MORE YOU DRAW, THE BETTER YOU'LL GET. DRAWING IS SUPPOSED TO BE **FUN** SO TRY NOT TO BE DISCOURAGED IF YOUR DRAWING DOESN'T LOOK LIKE YOU WANT IT TO.

HAPPY DRAWING!!!

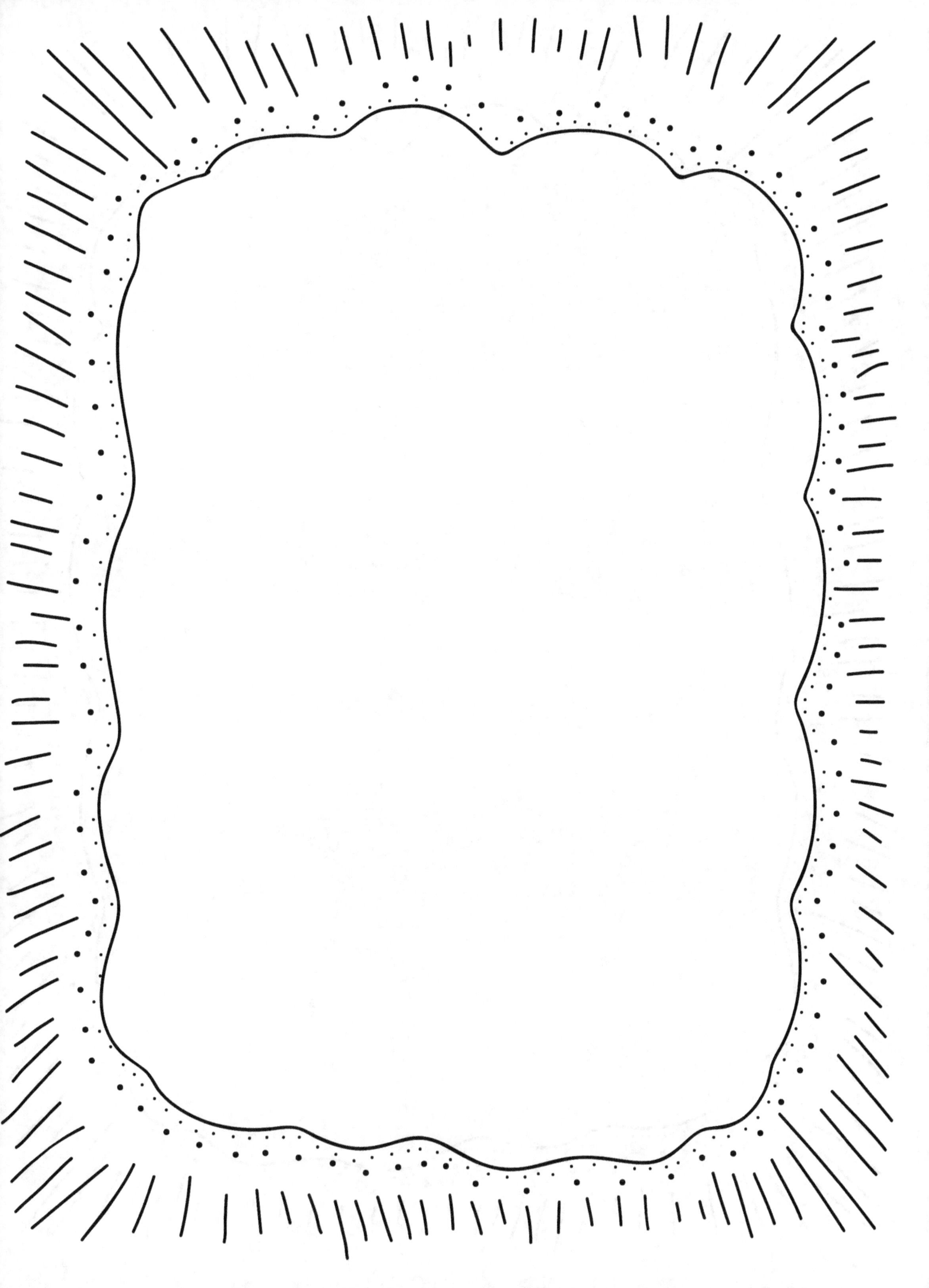

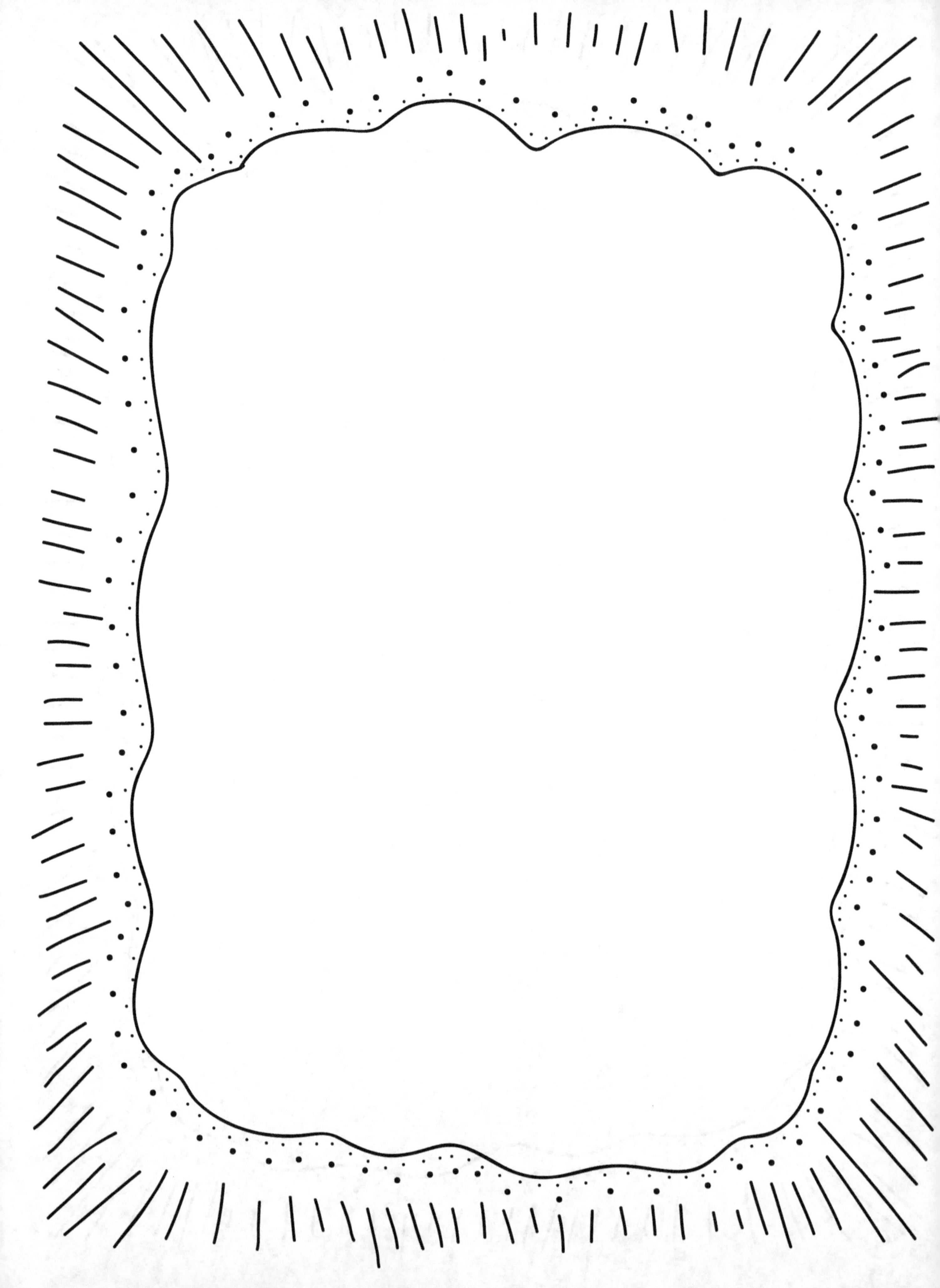

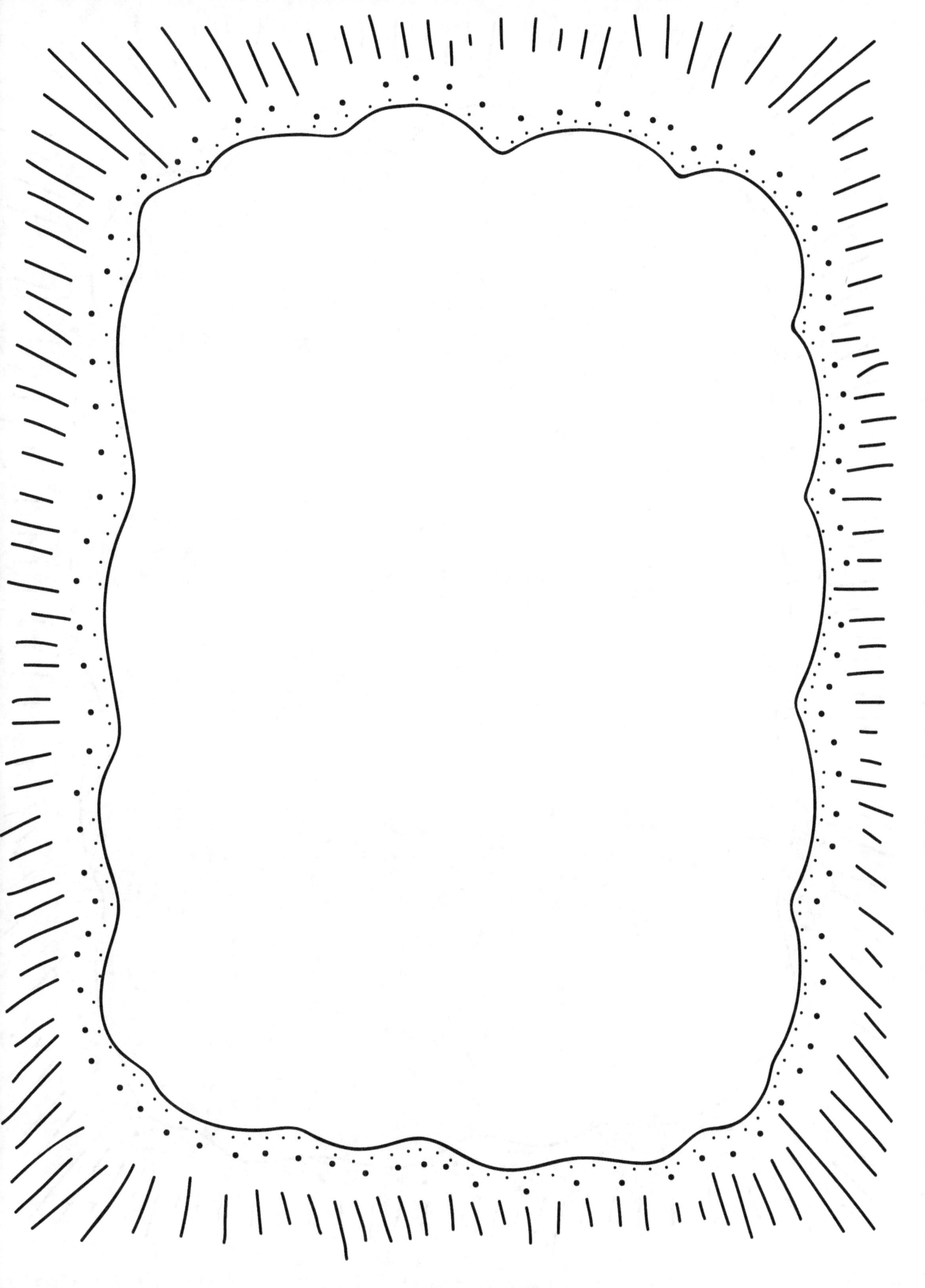

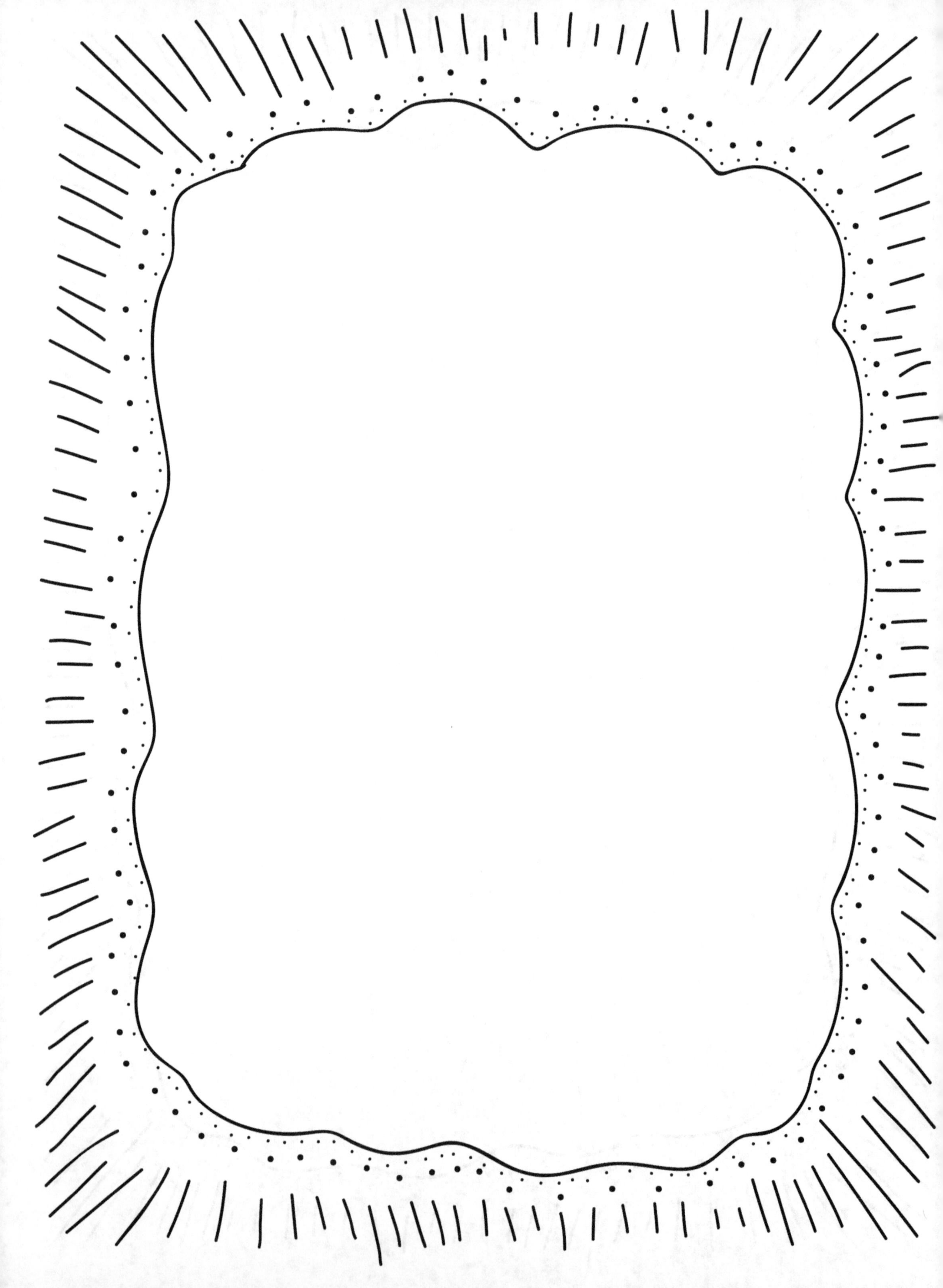

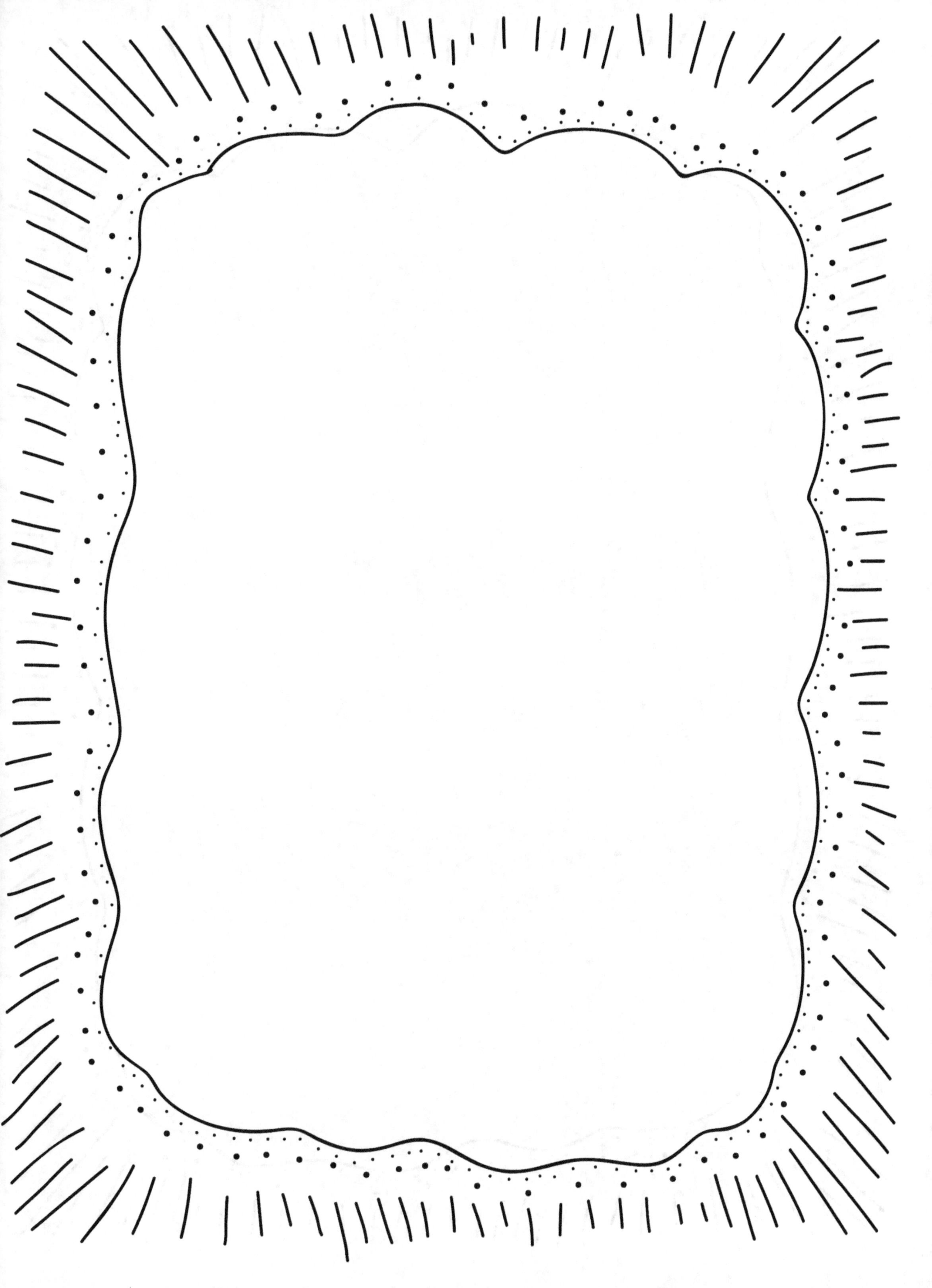

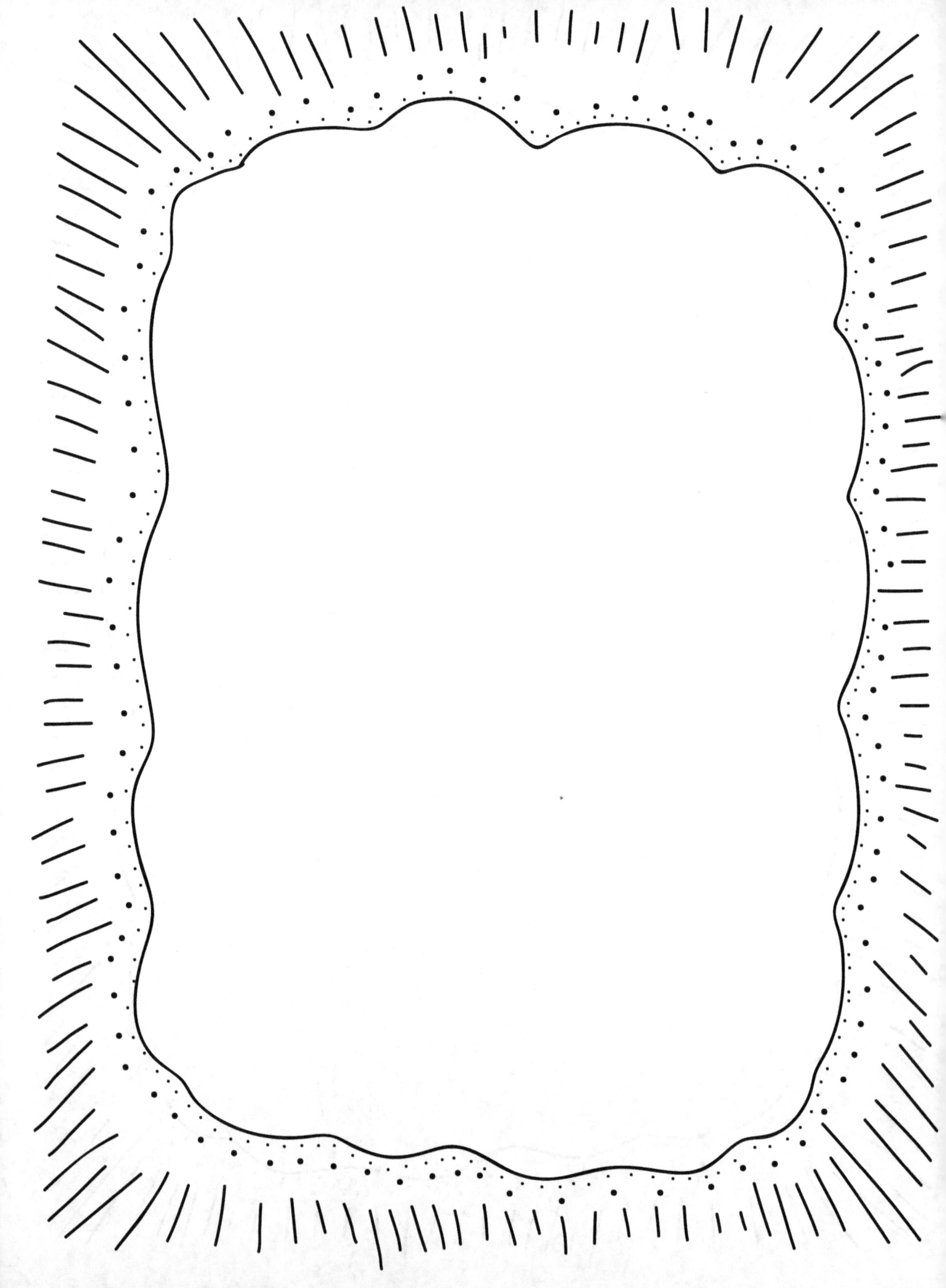

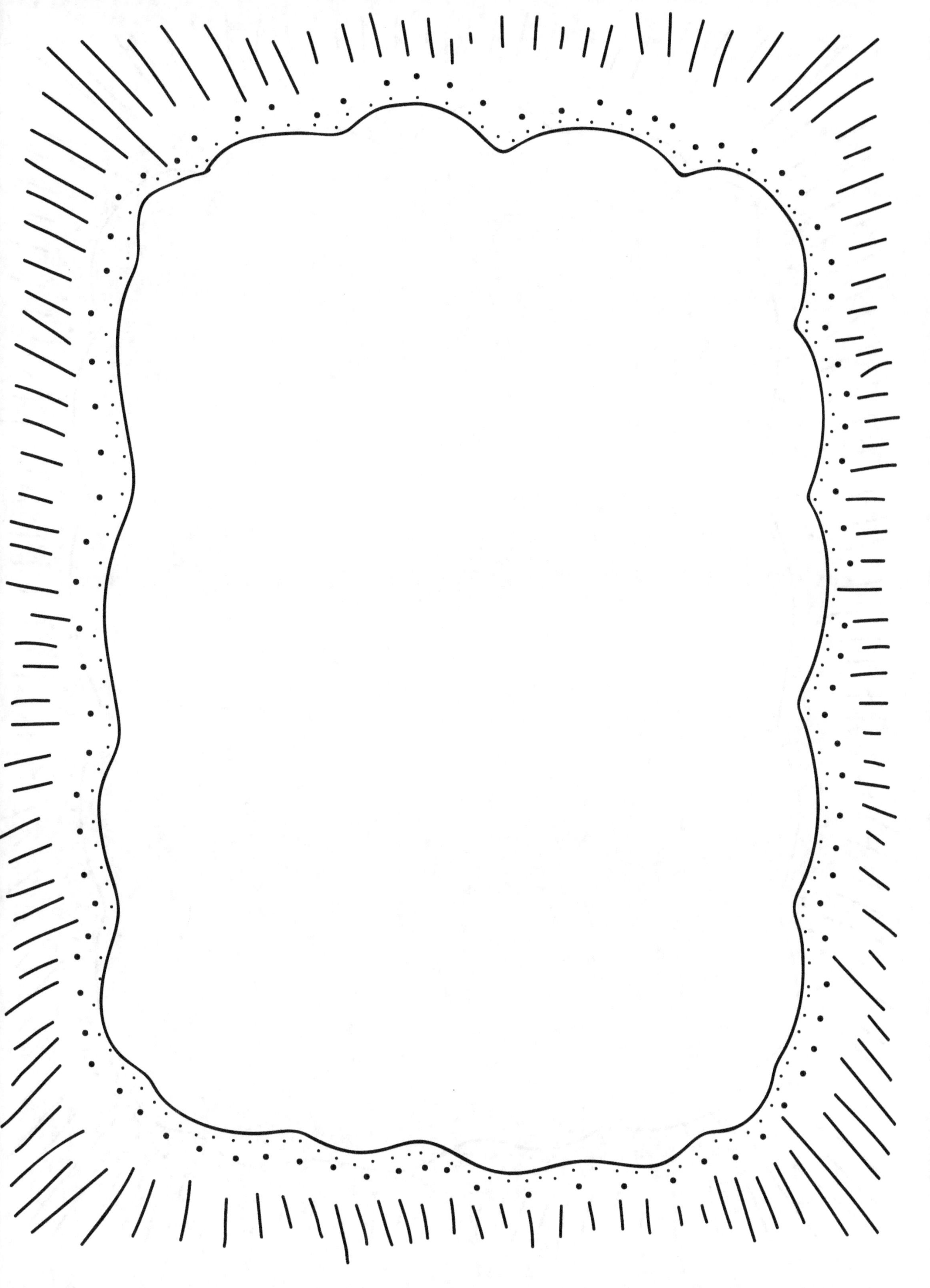

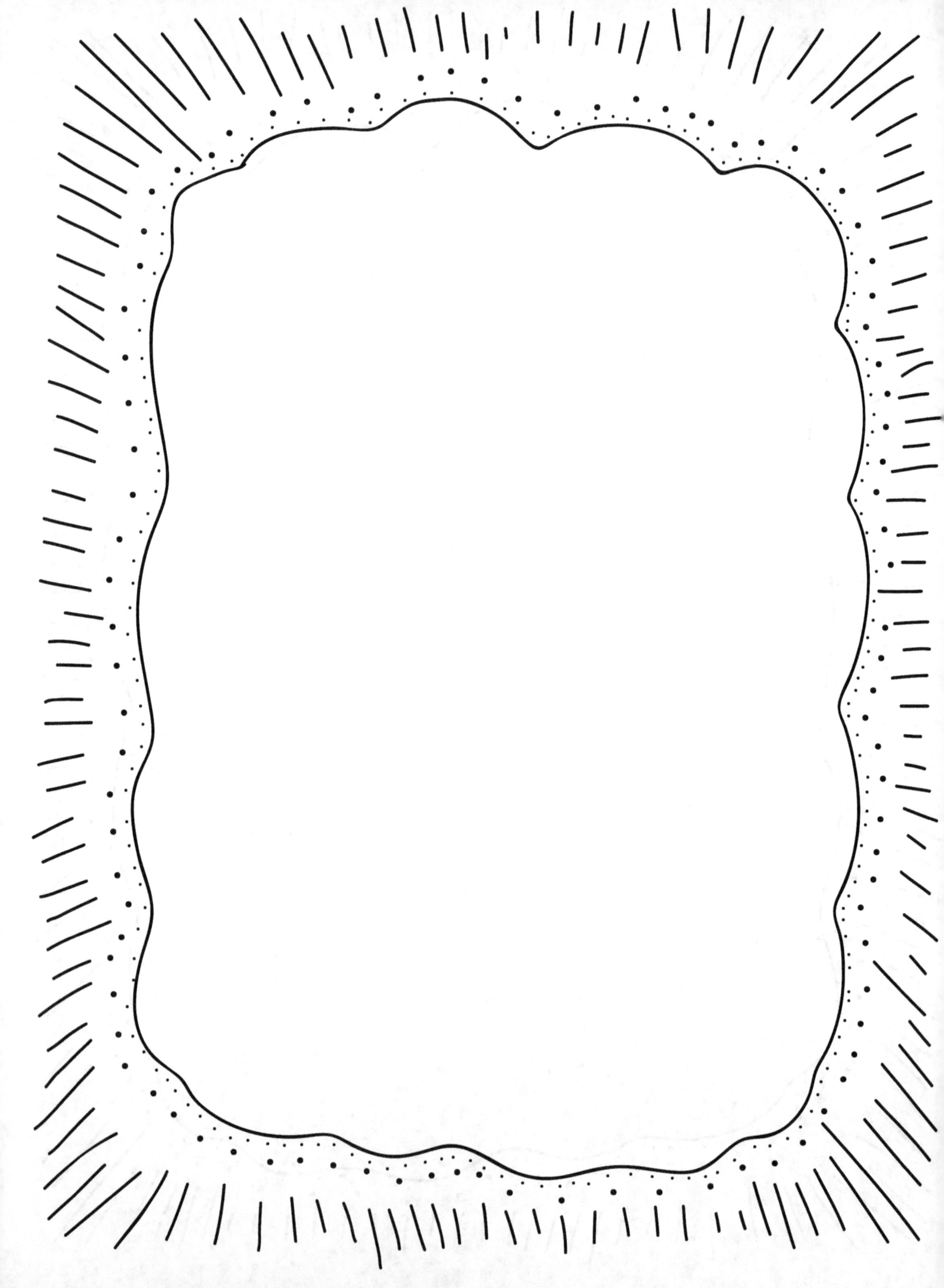

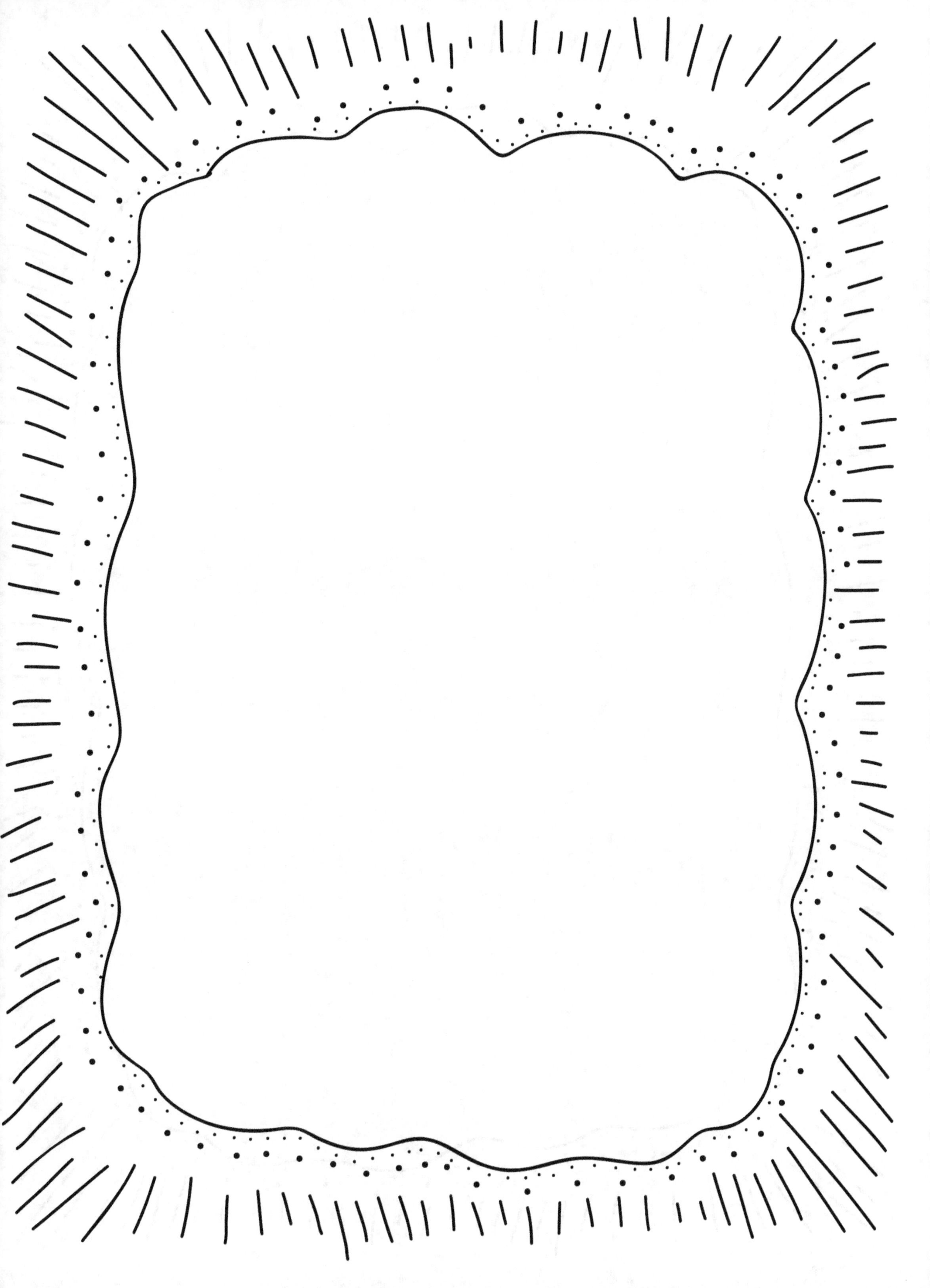

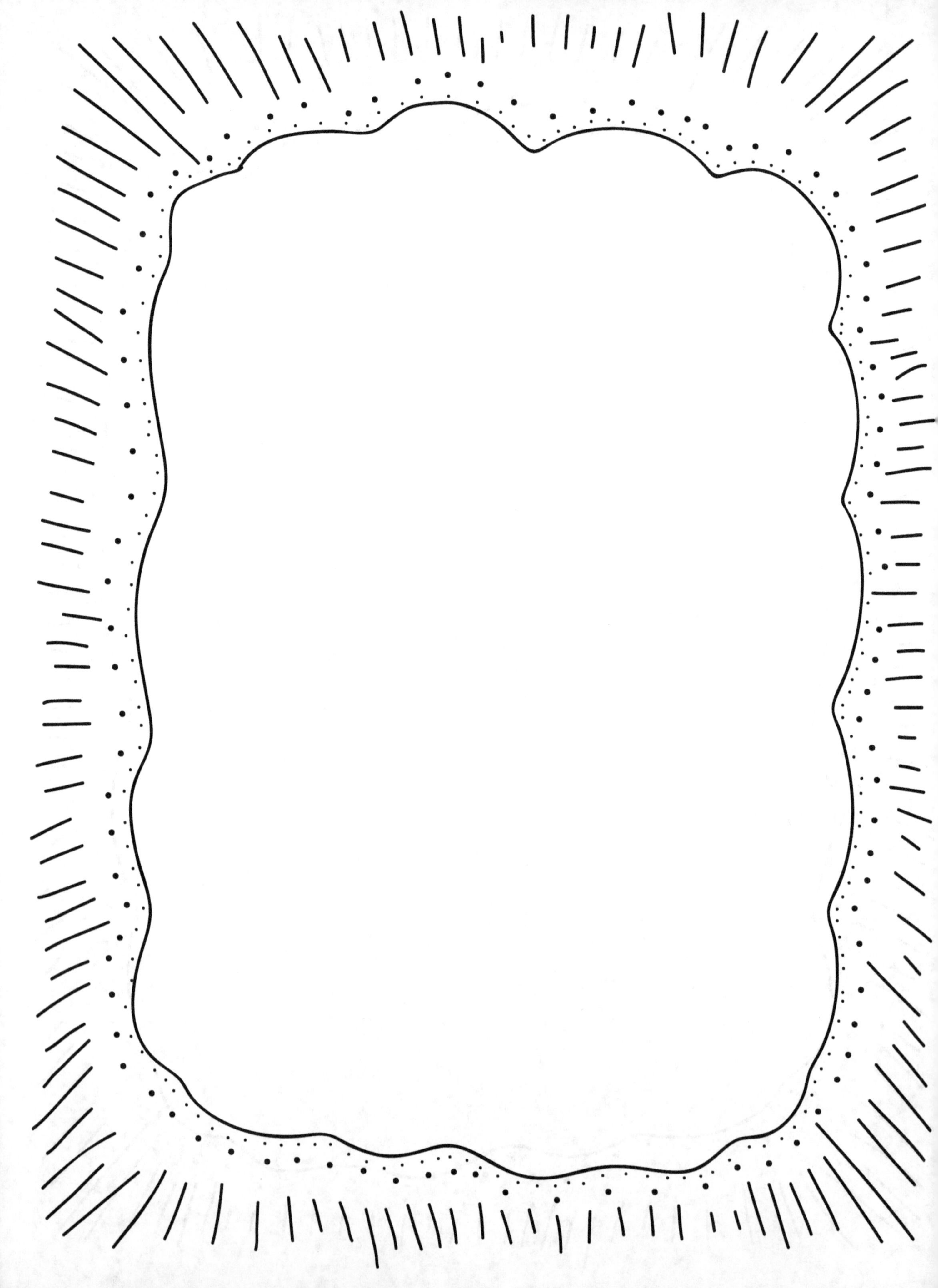

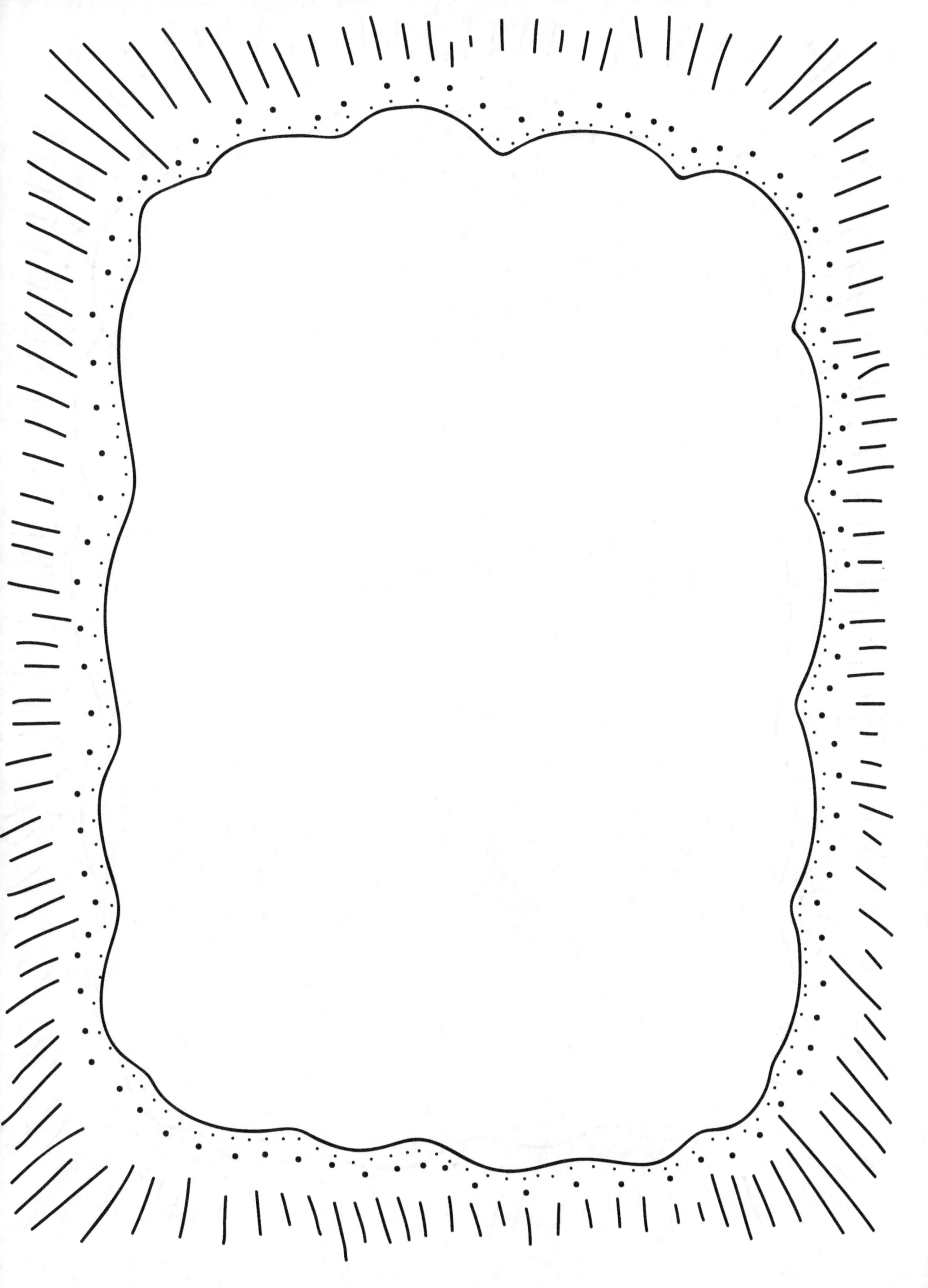

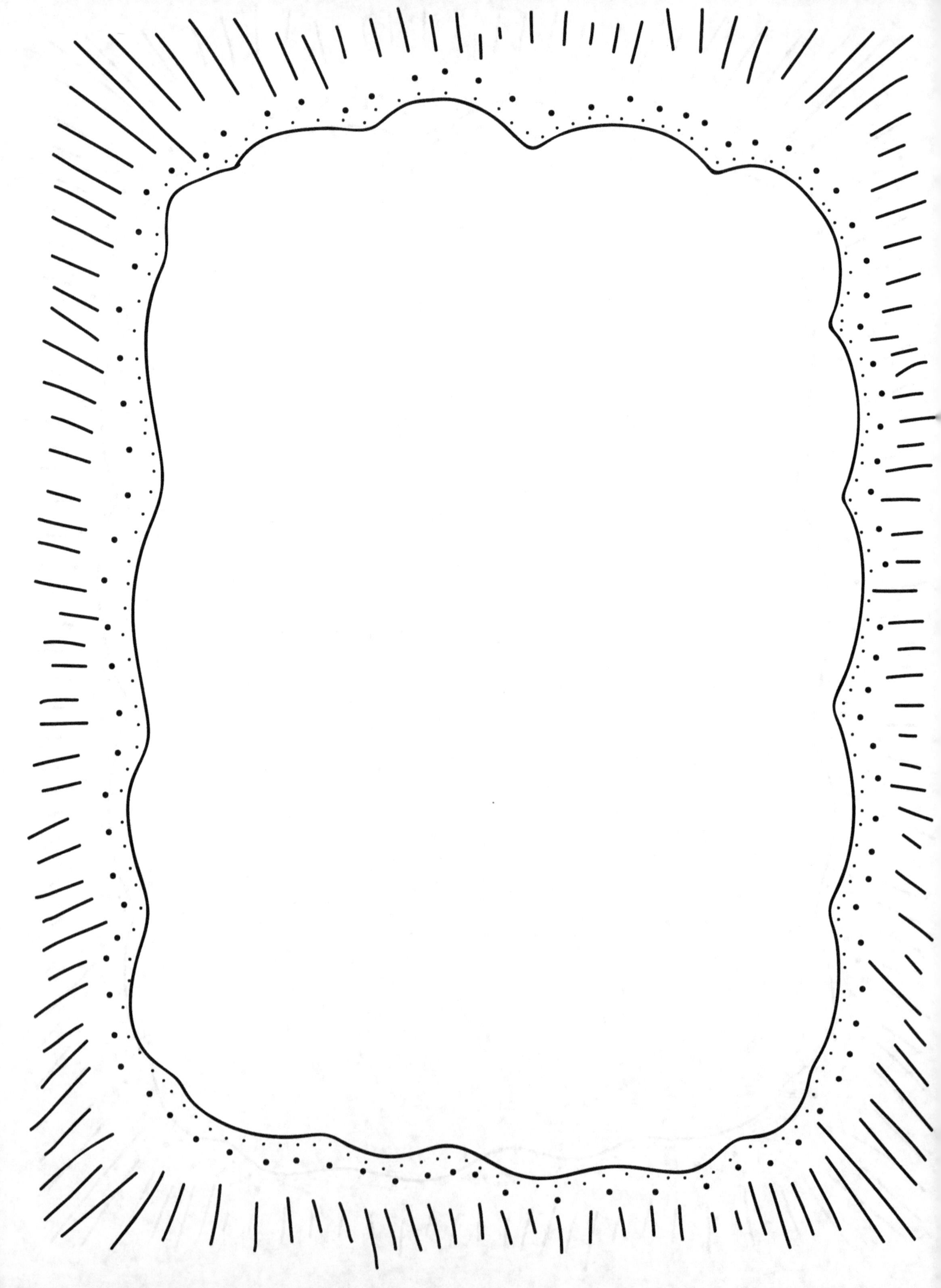

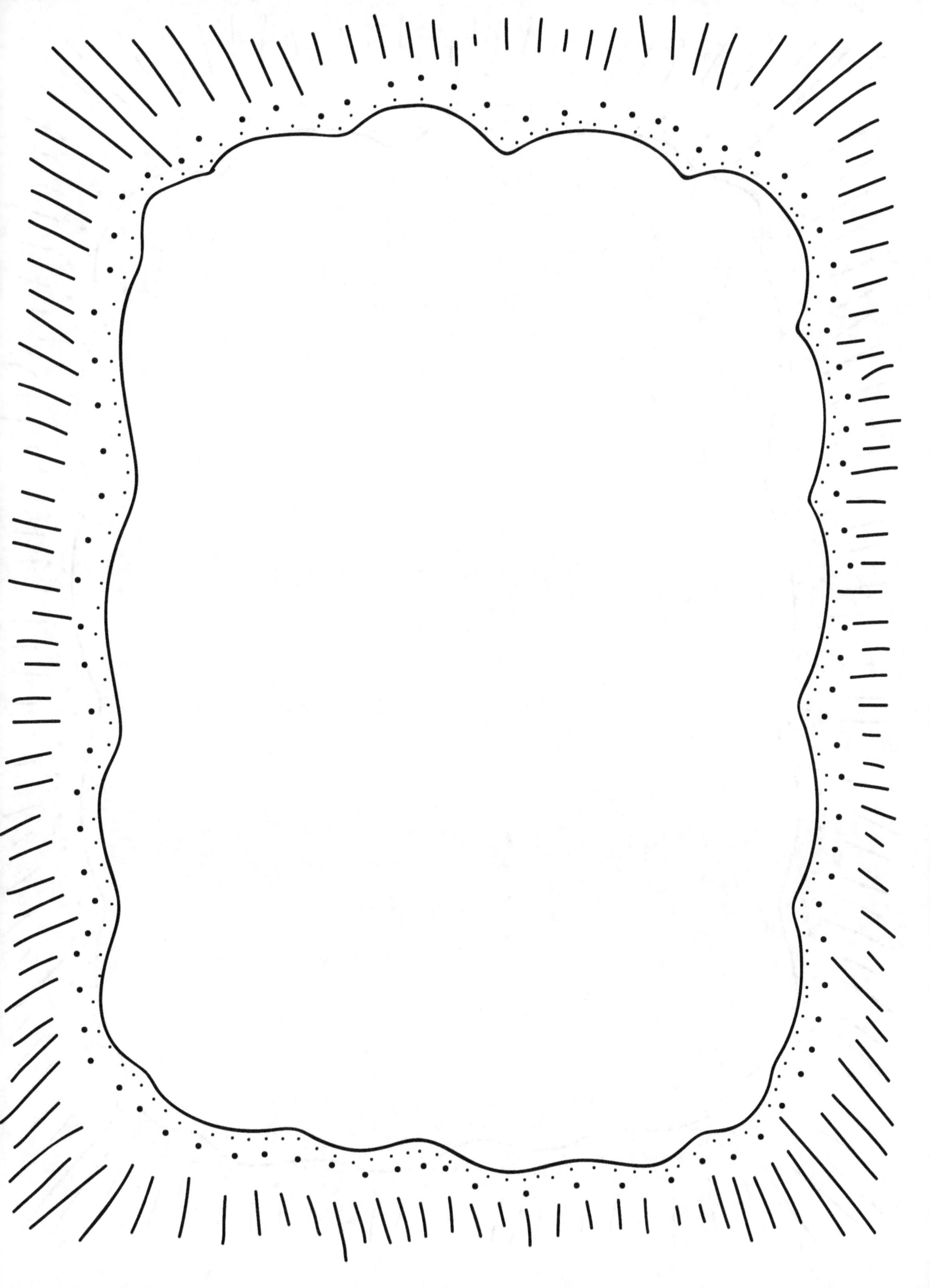

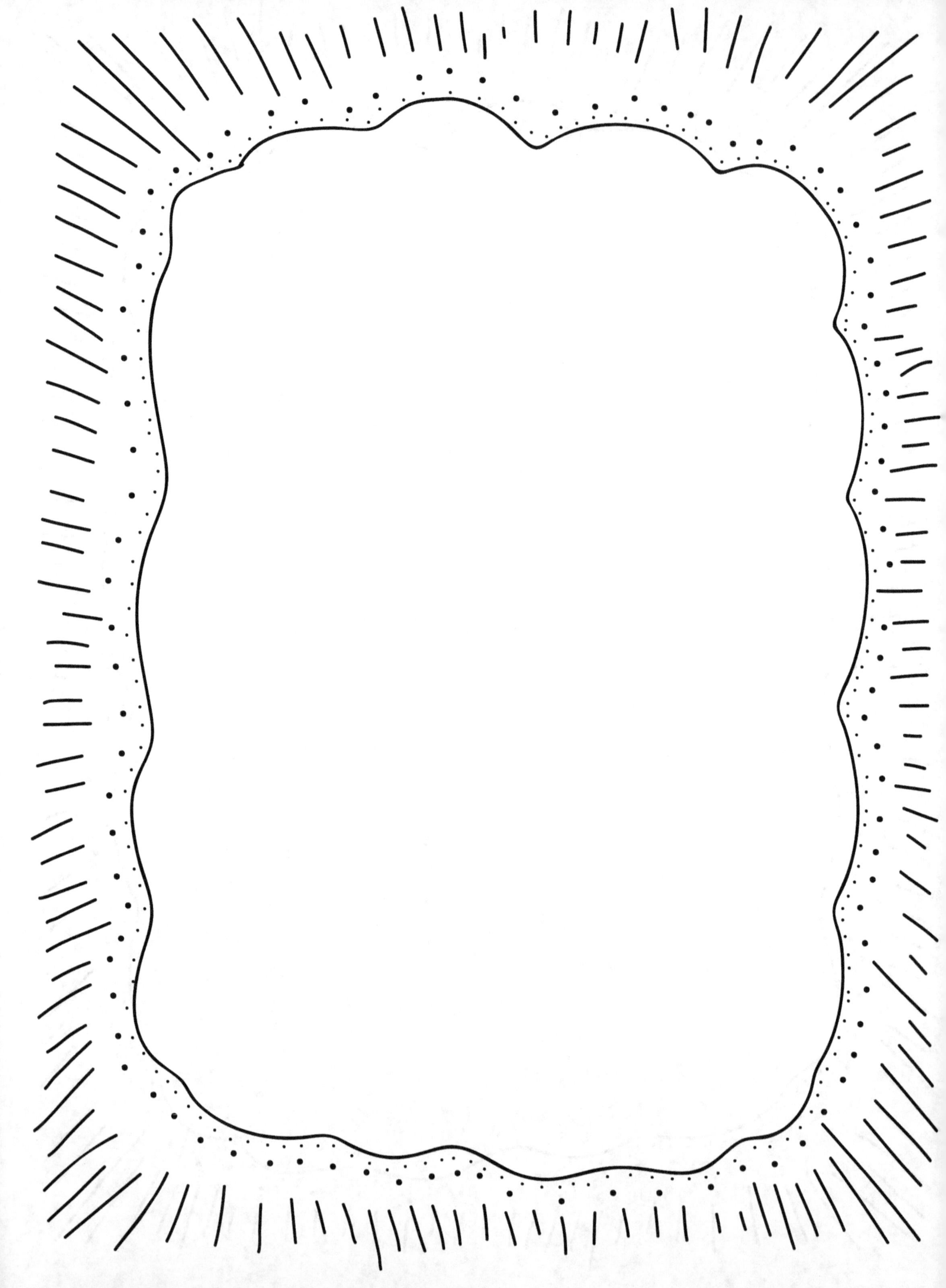

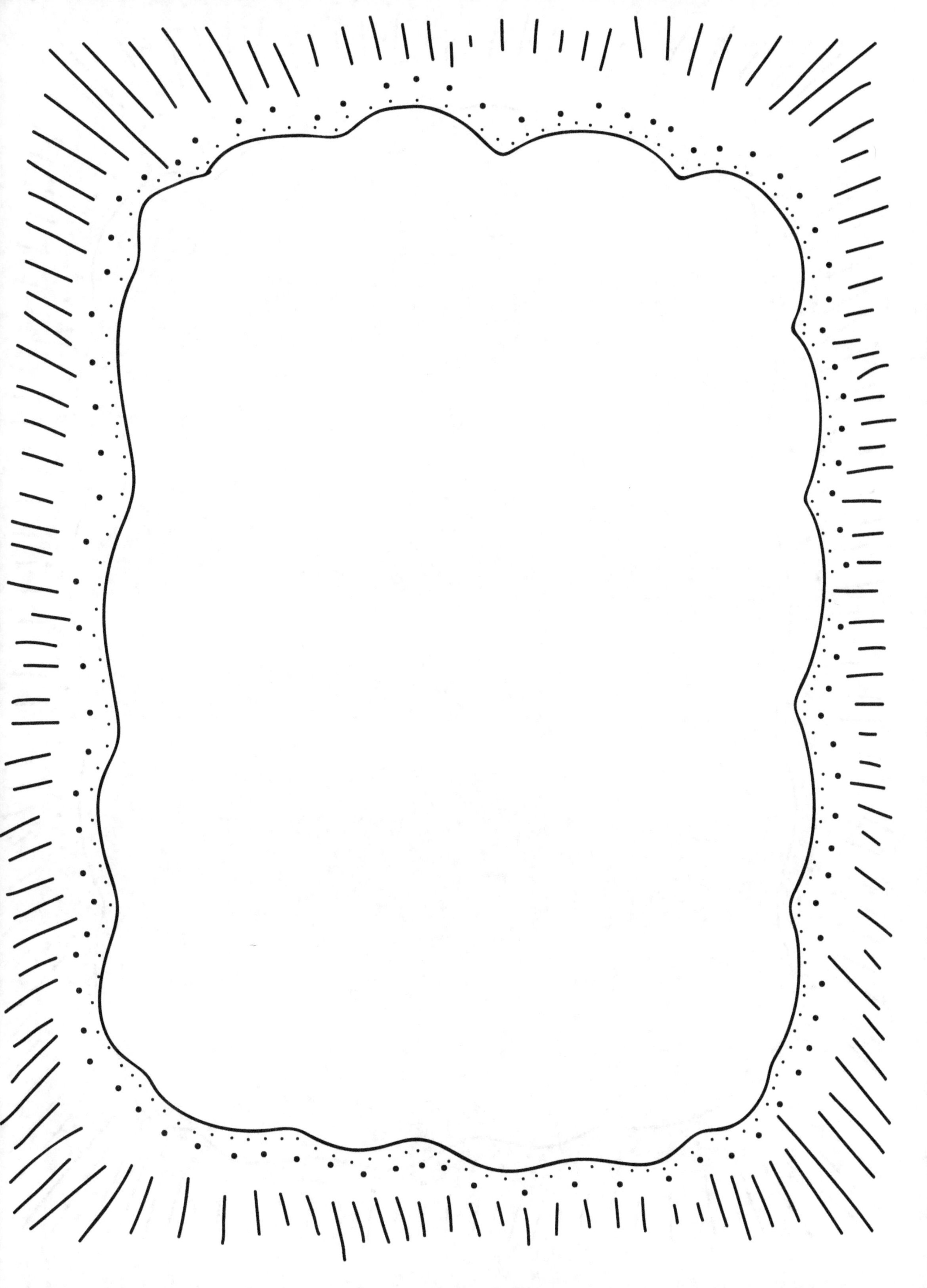

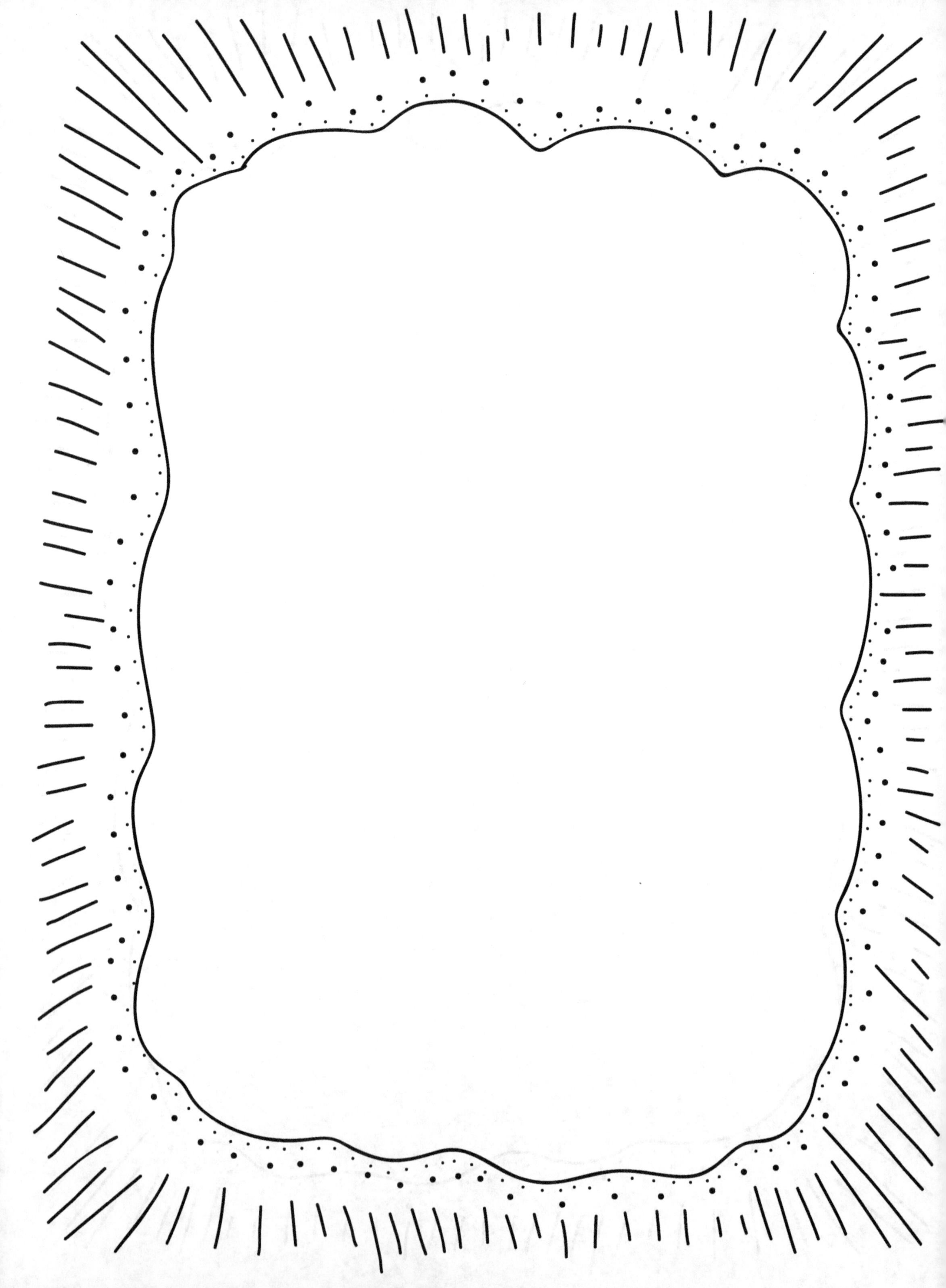

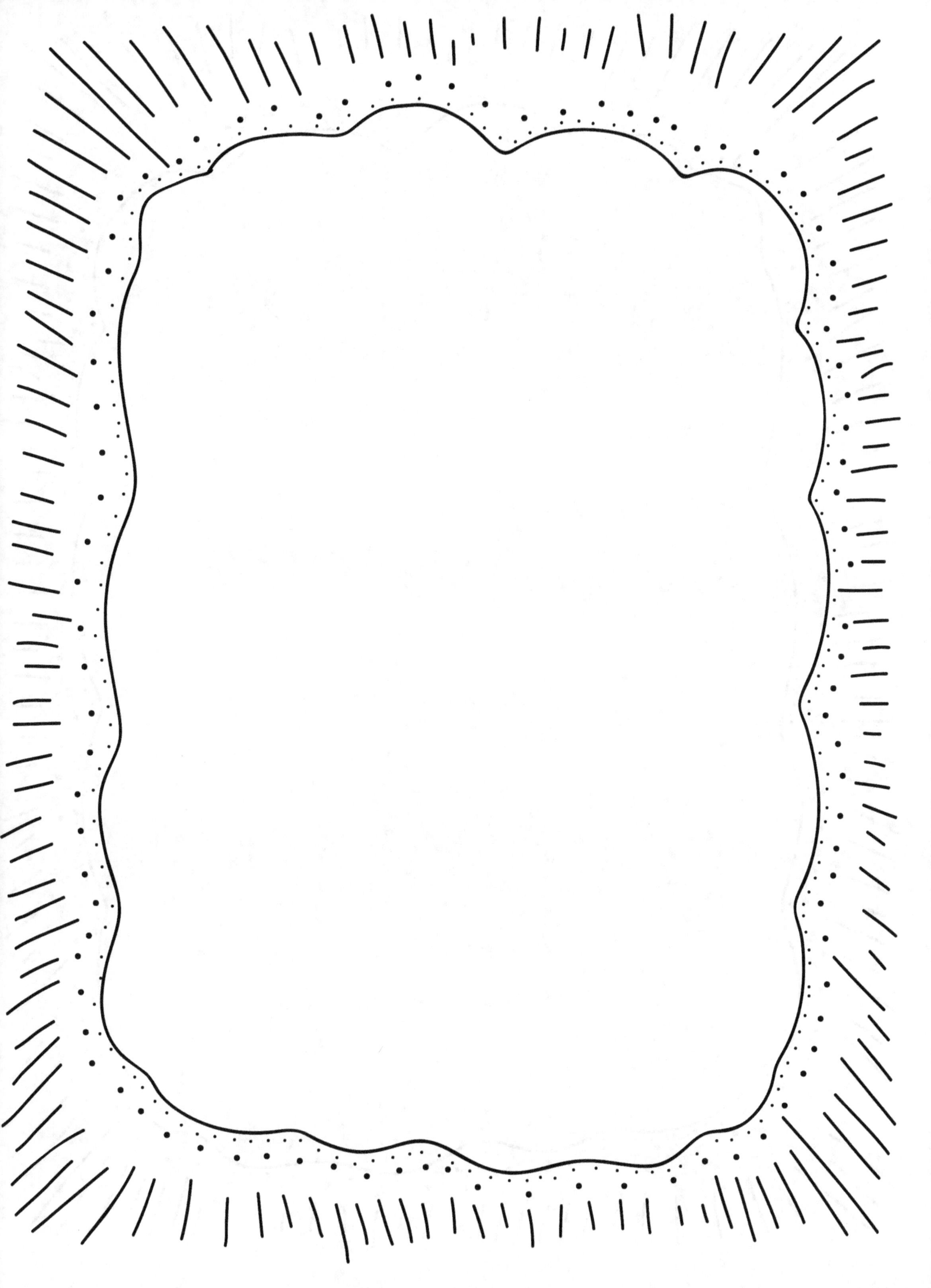

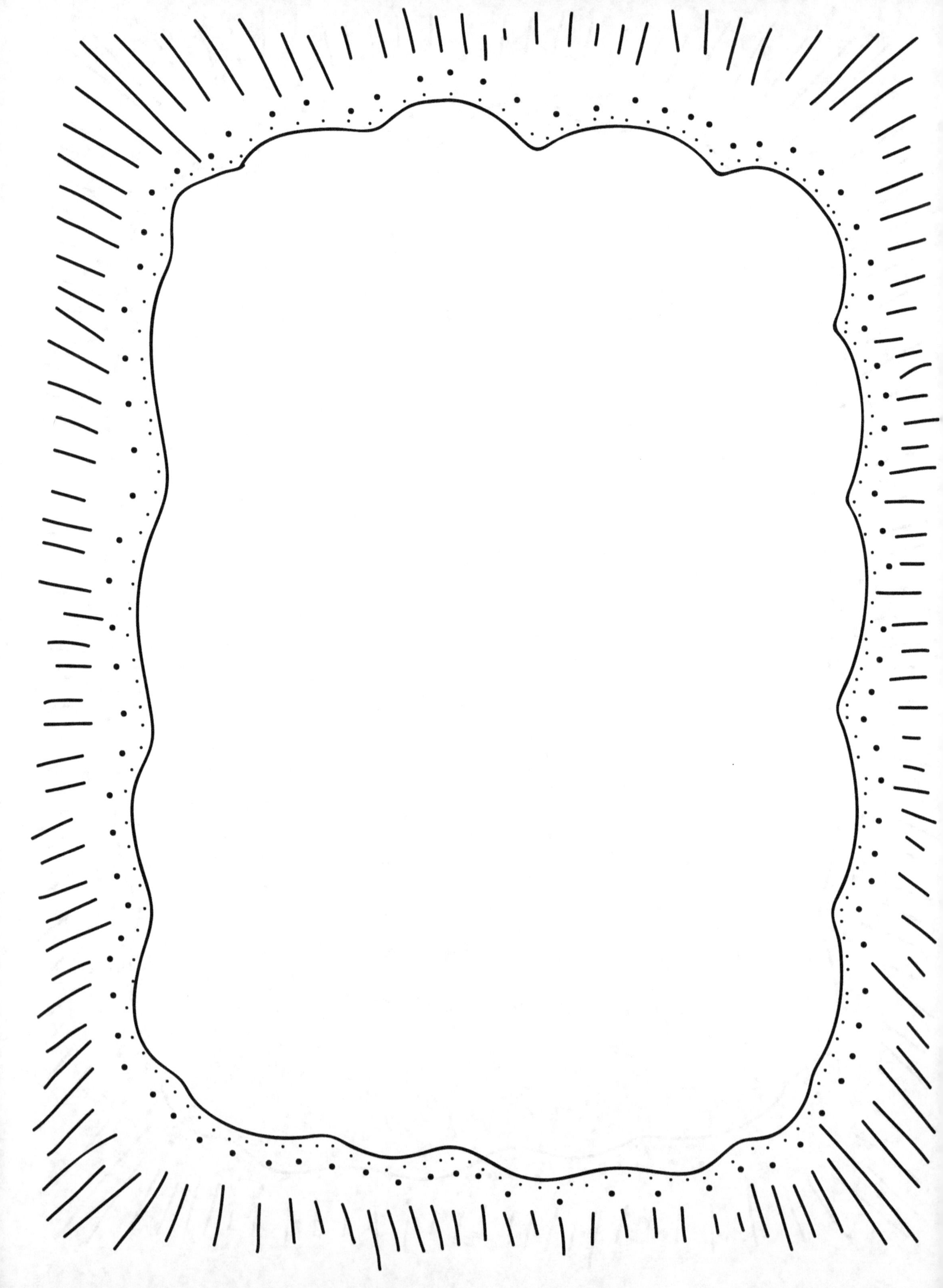